M000247598

A SPY IN THE SKY

With thanks to Mr Alan Philpott and Mrs Anne Philpott for their contribution to the writing and format of this book.

A SPY IN THE SKY

A PHOTOGRAPHIC RECONNAISSANCE SPITFIRE PILOT IN WWII

KENNETH B. JOHNSON

AIR WORLD

AIR WORLD

A SPY IN THE SKY
A Photographic Reconnaissance Spitfire Pilot in WWII

First published in Great Britain in 2019 by
Pen & Sword Air World
An imprint of
Pen & Sword Books Ltd
Yorkshire – Philadelphia

Copyright © Kenneth B. Johnson, 2019

ISBN 978 1 52676 156 9

The right of Kenneth B. Johnson to be identified as Author of this work has been
asserted by him in accordance with the Copyright, Designs and Patents Act 1988.

A CIP catalogue record for this book is available from the British Library.

All rights reserved. No part of this book may be reproduced or transmitted in any
form or by any means, electronic or mechanical including photocopying, recording
or by any information storage and retrieval system, without permission from the
Publisher in writing.

Typeset by Aura Technology and Software Services, India
Printed and bound in England by TJ International, Padstow, Cornwall, PL28 8RW

Pen & Sword Books Limited incorporates the imprints of Atlas, Archaeology,
Aviation, Discovery, Family History, Fiction, History, Maritime, Military, Military
Classics, Politics, Select, Transport, True Crime, Air World, Frontline Publishing,
Leo Cooper, Remember When, Seaforth Publishing, The Praetorian Press, Wharncliffe
Local History, Wharncliffe Transport, Wharncliffe True Crime and White Owl.

For a complete list of Pen & Sword titles please contact

PEN & SWORD BOOKS LIMITED
47 Church Street, Barnsley, South Yorkshire, S70 2AS, England
E-mail: enquiries@pen-and-sword.co.uk
Website: www.pen-and-sword.co.uk

Or
PEN AND SWORD BOOKS
1950 Lawrence Rd, Havertown, PA 19083, USA
E-mail: Uspen-and-sword@casematepublishers.com
Website: www.penandswordbooks.com

Contents

Preface

Constance Babington-Smith in her book Air Spy *wrote the story of Second World War intelligence gathering. Constance was a prominent intelligence officer of the Central Interpretation Unit of the Royal Air Force and United States Army Air Forces during the war. I was a 'spy' for both the RAF and USAAF during the Second World War.*

This is one story of how ordinary people from all walks of life came to the defence of their country in that war.

Imagine, yesterday you were 18 and today is 20 April 1943; you are photographing a Heinkel factory in the eastern part of Nazi Germany. It is cold, you are at 28,000 feet piloting an unarmed aircraft in crystal-clear daylight hundreds of miles from the safety of your base in England. If the imminent danger of being shot down by enemy fighters, and possibly killed, is not enough, you still have the problem of darkness to deal with when, or if, you cross back into England. Knowing that your fuel gauges will be hard on empty you will have to find a place to land, and landing your aircraft with no radio or cockpit lights in the pitch black of the English wartime blackout is tantamount to impossible. So what options will you have when your engine stops? Don't bother thinking about it. You got yourself into this situation, how are you going to get out of it?

Those 'magnificent men and their flying machines'! Would you have liked to have been one of them? This is the story of an eighteen-year-old who did become one. But being a 'Hero' is only in the eye of the beholder and it, too, has its ups and downs!

Chapter 1

The Country Calls

The Second World War had raged in Europe for more than a year. The country had been saved by those dashing Royal Air Force pilots during the recent Battle of Britain who were now considered heroes.

I had just turned eighteen. After experiencing enemy bombs dropping in Coventry it appeared it was time to volunteer for military service rather than wait to be conscripted into the Army (the trenches had no appeal for me!). I decided to join the Royal Air Force, thinking that I would be assigned to sweeping out hangars or some other unremarkable duties despite my childhood dream of becoming a pilot. But RAF pilots and aircrews were considered heroes as seen in pictures and newsreels; the thought that I could be one of them would be akin to thinking I could become a star in moving pictures.

On 20 February 1941 at RAF Station Cardington I was enlisted in the RAF as Aircraftman 2nd class Kenneth B. Johnson, service No. 1232125. Cardington was an old Royal Air Force base near Bedford, England. It was an inactive aerodrome, still boasting its past with two huge hangars, the larger one having housed the ill-fated R101 dirigible airship. It now, together with its mooring mast, stood forlorn.

Recruits arrived at RAF Cardington and were introduced into service life by being issued uniforms, given injections and vaccinations, and told 'You are now in the air force and will follow orders'. After learning how to polish buttons and maintain our appearance, we were sent home with vouchers authorising dentists to perform any dental work that might be required. The dental work was avoided by my being ordered to return after only four days. The question of why my presence was so urgently needed was answered when together with a mass of recruits we were put on a train and sent to the town of Weston-super-Mare. It being a well-known holiday resort, we hoped this was some sort of paid holiday.

Billeted in civilian homes we found what the holiday was to be; it was called 'Boot Camp'. Here we had military discipline drilled into us, together with being taught how to march and conduct ourselves as members of the Royal Air Force. This holiday tended to be rather strenuous due to the next few weeks being dedicated to physical training and exercises to sharpen our reflexes. In addition, our dental health was taken care of, and we found that it was not a painless experience.

The training did change us somewhat into the image of RAF airmen but we were shocked by the lack of ethics of a sergeant who said we could go on leave if we treated him right; we hoped it was an isolated incident and not typical of personnel of higher rank than ourselves. However, our stay in Weston-super-Mare did result in our being able to march in formation and left us feeling that we were now really airmen in the Royal Air Force. Putting the best and the worst of our boot camp training behind, we were given leave and sent home to await our new postings.

My posting was to RAF Station Sealand, located a few miles from Chester just across the border into Wales. It was an assignment to 'ground defence'; all I had to do to win the war was sit in a remote guard post with a Great War Lewis machine gun that probably did not work. However, the post did provide a grandstand view of an amphibious Walrus biplane landing on the airfield's grass with its undercarriage retracted. It was a surprise when the pilot opened the throttle and took off again and, after lowering the undercarriage, landed without any apparent damage to the aeroplane. The grandstand view of the flying activities did help to pass the time away and was a pleasant respite from bombing attacks.

Guard duty was not always fun, but the 'around the hangars' duty was good because no one knew where you were, and it provided the opportunity to examine many interesting aircraft, ranging from an old Hawker Hind to the new Bristol Beaufighter. I noticed the family resemblance of the fuselage of the Hind to that of the single-wing Hurricane fighter aircraft but, since Sydney Camm had designed both aircraft, the resemblance was not remarkable. The Marsh Lane guard duty was outside the airfield where a railway siding had once been; at night it was boring, but you had to stay alert in case anyone came to check (no one ever did). The guard duty to be avoided was at the officers' gate; this duty was only done at night and after the usual 'who goes there?' it was necessary to identify the rank of any approaching officer to determine whether to salute or present arms as required by military regulations. It was necessary to salute an officer with the rank of squadron leader and below by slapping the butt of the rifle with the right hand and for officers holding the rank of wing commander and above to present arms. The rank identification was a problem on a dark night in the wartime blackout. But there was no danger of anyone getting hurt since we did not mount bayonets and the rifles did not present a threat either since no ammunition was issued for the duty; to this day I look back on that duty as being a sketch from some sort of variety show. On the 25-yard firing range I made a name for myself; I had been issued with a Ross P14 rifle and with it I became the best shot of all the airmen in the group, although the sergeant in charge pointed out that I had no right to be the best shot since I ignored the tenets of good marksmanship by closing my eyes and snatching the trigger instead of squeezing it. This criticism did not faze me; I was still the best shot and I am sure the enemy would have cringed if they had known about it.

Sealand aerodrome in the early part of the war was an Elementary Flying Training School (EFTS) where student pilots were taught to fly in DH 82a Tiger Moths; to me the aeroplanes did look rather nice and probably were fun to fly. When an officer's car broke down just outside the aerodrome, with the left front wheel canted at an angle, I knew what needed to be done and volunteered to fix it. After jacking up the 1934 Hillman Minx car, I knocked the king-pin back into place and the repair was done. The officer thanked me for having solved his problem and, thinking he might be a flight instructor, I plucked up courage and asked if there was a chance of getting a ride in one of the aeroplanes. Of course, I never did get a ride, which was hardly surprising as I was only a rather dirty, uncouth airman second class (the lowest rank in the RAF). But being around trainer aeroplanes and the officer pilots who flew them did make the image of RAF heroes a little more realistic.

Standing guard at what was known as the railway gate at the back of the old married quarters on the opposite side of the road past the aerodrome, I found carved into the wood a four-line ditty, which read as follows:

> They serve, even those who only stand and wait,
> So said the men who rule our wretched fate,
> We thought they meant beside a fighting crate,
> Not this bloody useless railway gate.

The ditty was amusing but I wondered if whoever carved it into the gate was being made to do guard duty before being trained as an aircrew member? I dismissed the thought; obviously they would not treat potential aircrew members like that.

It was rare for anyone to own a car and for an RAF AC2 to own one was almost unheard of, but I did have one and was given permission to bring my

1933 Ford Eight onto the station. Claiming to be an atheist I missed church parade one Sunday, hitchhiked home, and returned driving my car.

One evening we were served something that had become unknown to us since the start of the war – ice cream. It was served in the airmen's mess at the evening meal. We wondered if this unusual circumstance could be the harbinger of doom? We were more used to hardtack biscuits (which were literally left over from the Great War in sealed boxes) than ice cream, but our question was soon to be answered.

Three of us were told that we were being transferred to RAF Station Ouston; however, wartime security prevented us from being told where RAF Station Ouston was, and no one else seemed to know the location of RAF Station Ouston or how to find it.

We thought that it was perhaps some kind of official secret, but we were authorised to drive to Ouston in my car and, armed with this lack of information, we decided hopefully to try and find it on our own. Carefully scrutinising any pre-war road maps that we could find, we decided that, of the two Oustons we found, one marked by a little dot on the map near Hadrian's Wall near Newcastle-on-Tyne in Northumberland was the more likely; it did seem more logical as the other Ouston appeared to be in a place so remote that we might not be able to find it at all. After driving many hours and becoming hopelessly lost in the wartime blackout with no signposts to guide us (all signposts had been removed, apparently to prevent us from getting to where we were supposed to go) even if we did know where to go. We eventually gave up trying to find this elusive RAF Station Ouston; I was too tired to drive any longer and decided we would have to sleep in the car until morning with the hope that we would perhaps have better luck in daylight the next day. Waking up in the early morning light we were shocked to see the tail of an RAF aircraft sticking up behind a thick hedge just a few feet away. Well, some days you just get lucky; it was not only the dot on the map marked Ouston it was also RAF Station Ouston; our guess had been correct. Despite the uncertainty and discomfort of getting to this new posting, being in the RAF seemed to be much better than conscription into the Army. We felt lucky that we had stumbled upon the correct location or we might have been considered AWOL (Absent Without Official Leave) for not having reported in at the new posting on time, being conscripted into the Army would perhaps not have seemed quite such an unattractive alternative. Having reported in at the guardroom we went through the signing in routine, obtaining signatures at about a dozen different places (and issued a tin tea mug), we were totally unaware of the location of each of the places where we had to sign in, but it did teach us to find our way around the station. RAF Station Ouston was brand new and had been created from scratch with new buildings, hangars and runways replacing what had been open fields just a few months before. It had good barrack accommodation and a surprisingly good mess with excellent food. At the midday meal, we even had music; an Air Force band played, among other things, Glen Miller's 'Tuxedo Junction', sounding just the same as the Glen Miller Orchestra. We felt that life in the Royal Air Force was not at all bad.

Chapter 2

The Surprise

We now felt that we had completed our training and, having checked in, the next thing was to find out what our duties were. To say that we were surprised would be an understatement when we were told that we were now aircrew in training and were to wear a white flash in the fronts of our forage caps to signify this. Before my induction into the RAF I had been interviewed by a review board for what I thought might be for aircrew selection. I attended the aircrew selection boards twice and was told I had failed the interviews – 'twice'! So it appeared this posting was an administrative mistake that would be corrected when the records were sorted out. Although I had admired and thought of those dashing brave Royal Air Force pilots as gods flying high in the sky, it was beyond any stretch of my imagination that I could ever be one. I suppose I was scared, I had a low esteem of myself and was used to being looked down upon as always wrong. I certainly was not a member of the upper class and my education was only enough to qualify me to deliver bread. Class distinction would certainly preclude me from any position of responsibility due to the circumstance of my birth. But, in the meantime, I had no option but to just sit back and enjoy being paid for doing nothing.

There were approximately thirty of us in the group and we felt pampered. No one shouted at us and our only duties appeared to be taking turns at marching the others as if we were drill sergeants; I guessed this was to instill command capabilities, although no one told us that. The only demand made on us, in the company of many other airmen, was to lift the wing of a Blenheim aircraft and release a wheel stuck in the mud; with a shout of 'two-six' the wing was easily lifted enabling the aircraft to be moved. It was annoying when our sojourn at RAF Ouston was cut short by a new posting to RAF Station Catterick Bridge. There seemed to be no imminent threat to the elevated esteem which we now enjoyed as 'aircrew in training' and the move to RAF Station Catterick was interesting; like most pre-war aerodromes it did not have runways and aircraft operated from a grass surface. A Czechoslovakian Spitfire squadron apparently on rest was stationed there and the only flying activities appeared to be by the squadron conducting training flights. A single-engine Wellesley bomber aircraft stood on the hard standing; it was interesting because it had been designed using Professor Barnes Wallis's geodetic structure, the type of structure that was later incorporated into the design of the Wellington bomber (better known in those days as a 'Wimpy' after the Popeye cartoon character J. Wellington Wimpy).

Although one might imagine that this now expanded group of (upstanding?) young men comprised of both British and colonials (the term 'colonials' referring to anyone who came from a place other than the British Isles) was the best that Britain had to offer as potential aircrews. Among them were two good guys, Cyrus 'Sunshine' Stott from Lancashire and Peter Tew from Hull; both were great company although Peter did wear shiney silk gold-coloured Chinese pyjamas. On the other hand, Cyrus, who claimed to be from the United States, had apparently thought that life in the RAF was preferable to being a private in the Army (he was found to be a deserter from the Canadian Army). But the group appeared to be made up of questionable characters, some of whom were downright unsavoury and gave the appearance of having been given an early release from prison rather than potential aircrew. One can commiserate with the task of Sergeant Anis who was in charge of what appeared to be, and was, a motley group. I could not understand what the game was, could these really be what the Royal Air Force considered to be potential aircrew members. Surely potential aircrew members were refined and recruited from the elite of society? No, they certainly could not be destined for any role like that!

I was called 'Snake-hips', a nickname apparently styled after the American bandleader by the same name, Ken 'Snake-hips' Johnson, who had been killed when a German bomb destroyed the Café de Paris in London. But in conformance with the saying 'It's not who you are, it's what they say you are' my reputation did not improve by being called 'Snake-hips'. I drove to Leicester in the company of Sunshine Stott and an airman nicknamed 'Tiger' on a weekend pass. I yielded to a request by Tiger to borrow the car to go on to Coventry with his promise to pick up Sunshine, who was staying with me, and me in front of St Mark's Church on Belgrave Road in Leicester at 2:00am on the following Monday morning, which would give us sufficient time to return to Catterick by the 8:30am deadline. I learned the lesson of not to trust anyone in this company of unreformed gangsters. We could still be standing there waiting; Tiger failed to pick us up. This breach of trust forced us to have to hitchhike back to Catterick. Of course Tiger, driving my car, arrived back on time but having to hitchhike caused us to be half an hour late. However, there was a bright side. Instead of being put on a charge, our punishment was informal and we were confined to camp the following weekend and told to spend the time working in the tin room. The mess hall was brand new and the tin room was automated, leaving us with little work to do. The easygoing mess sergeant told us to relax and eat whatever we wanted and have a pleasant weekend. Being on jankers wasn't at all bad.

But being confined to camp for the weekend, I was unaware that I was being taken advantage of again. Tiger had taken my car without my permission or knowledge and driven it to Newcastle on Tyne. This time he had run over a little old lady and broken her arm; he also had had a one-car accident and bent the front axle. I was appalled that he had taken advantage of me again. I may have been a slow learner, but I made sure the injured lady was taken care of fully and straightened the front axle of the car in the station's blacksmith shop. Although not being considered anything other than a stupid kid, I always honoured my responsibilities despite their being caused by another person who apparently lacked any ethics at all. I may have only been a young boy, but I had a deep feeling of disgust that anyone could behave in such an uncaring and irresponsible manner. But that was not the only problem I had to cope with as someone stole the ignition coil from my car, although why anyone would steal an ignition coil, which could be so easily replaced, was beyond me. I merely walked to a local garage and bought a used coil for a half-crown (12.5p) and the car was running again. But that was not the end of the story; Sergeant Anis brought me up on a charge of stealing the coil from another car. Luckily, the officer who heard the charge could see through what was happening and dismissed the charge. When I was posted to a new assignment, Sergeant Anis, who by then had seen through the false information that the troublemakers had been feeding him, was good enough to provide me with an apology. I was still at that time an 'Erk', an AC2 (the lowest rank in the RAF) and the apology from the sergeant made me feel that a cloud had been lifted from over my head; I was learning the hard way that there were many people who could not be trusted. I was becoming a little less naïve but could not believe that these people could possibly be trusted as members of an aircrew, except possibly in the Luftwaffe!

During the time at Catterick I was slowly growing up, learning a great deal about the quality or lack of it in some; I found that even an Army officer could make mistakes. It was raining on a Sunday afternoon when out of the gloom pieces of an aircraft started falling from the base of the low cloud, but no one had heard any sound of aircraft engines. The pieces fell to the north of RAF Station Catterick and were followed a few minutes later by a solitary parachute. I got in my car and raced to the site where the pieces fell; apart from some gruesome remains, a large part of a cockpit lay nearby. The cockpit had four throttles and a large 'B' in the centre of the control column yokes, I immediately identified it as the wreckage of an early American Boeing B-17 but an Army officer who arrived at the site dismissed my identification and identified it as a Bristol aeroplane, although the Bristol Aeroplane Company did not make a four-engine aircraft at that time or put a logo in the centre of the control columns. I realised that Army officers were not as familiar with aircraft recognition as members of the RAF, but I had become smart enough not to contradict him, although it did seem incorrect that my observation should have been be dismissed without any consideration of the reason for my having made it.

On a warm afternoon a few days later, while trying to stay awake during a lecture, the sounds of Chopin's 'Funeral March' drifted in from the funerals of the crew of the ill-fated B-17. The crew had been comprised of American civilian aviators, except for the parachutist who, it transpired, was a Royal Air Force medical officer holding the rank of wing commander. At the board of enquiry, the wing commander gave evidence that it was an evaluation flight that had been flying at 30,000 feet but had no recollection of anything untoward occurring; apparently, he had been rendered unconscious and had no idea how he came to be wearing a parachute; his mind was blank until regaining consciousness dangling from a parachute in the rain. If the cause of the crash was ever determined I never became aware of it. Another accident, but with a happy ending, happened when a Spitfire landed smoothly but, as it slowed down, the right-hand wheel came off; fortunately on the soft ground the aircraft just slewed round with apparently little damage and with no injuries to the pilot, but things like this made me realise that flying was not safe and could be hazardous.

The deaths of the B-17 crew saddened me and I recognised that I had been living in a fool's paradise, realising that if the mistake in my records had not been a mistake I could end up in an aeroplane with all the associated dangers. But with the bunch of rogues that I was now in the midst of I began to think that perhaps a mistake had not been made in assigning me to aircrew training; the need must have been great to include such unsavoury characters as I was now with. We were probably fated for training as air gunners as few exhibited having more than a minimal education.

I was told to take my car home when I was posted from Catterick to another assignment where I would not be permitted to have a car, but before taking the car back to Leicester I stopped at the NAAFI and bought some Players Weights cigarettes for my brother. Although I did not smoke, I knew cigarettes were scarce and hard to obtain and since the NAAFI had some available it seemed the proper thing to do for my brother who did smoke. He was now a private in the Leicestershire Regiment stationed at Glen Parva Barracks just outside Leicester, a location that made it easy to deliver the cigarettes while on my way to my new posting.

The new posting was to Babbacombe in Devon, near Torquay, and the airmen in the group I was now among appeared to be better educated and displayed much better character traits than the ex-cons at Catterick. This posting was more like a holiday than fulfilling military duties; it was not at a regular RAF station and we were billeted in pre-war hotels with nothing to do but wait for further instructions. Babbacombe was pleasant and overlooked Oddicombe beach with the funicular tram from the promenade still operating. Observing an airman wearing pilot's wings without a badge of rank on his sleeve indicated that his rank was only that of an AC2, the same rank that I held and it made me wonder how an AC2 could be a qualified RAF pilot since all aircrew held at least the rank of sergeant so why was he not at least a sergeant (was this a shade of what could happen if you did not toe some sort of line)? But thoughts or concern about such matters in this idyllic setting were more of what we were doing there and what was in store for us, but it appeared that we were there for some type of specialised training. But what specialised training was it?

It just kept getting better. After a few lazy days our holiday accommodations were changed from Babbacombe to the luxurious Grand Hotel in Torquay which had been taken over by the RAF to accommodate airmen attending ITW (Initial Training Wing). Although the hotel had been stripped of its peacetime luxury, it still came as a shock to stay in such a hotel, or even visit Torquay. We found that our enrolment in the Initial Training Wing meant that, if we were paying attention, we would be entertained by attending many 'useful' lectures. One lecture held at the Roslyn Hall Hotel taught us to recognise and correct the stoppages of the Vickers gas-operated machine gun. We were also provided with intimate knowledge of the Great War Lewis machine gun. These guns were from a war more than twenty years before. Were air gunners still using these weapons? I was beginning to wonder if they were still using Spads and Nieuports as fighter aircraft; but, not to worry, there were more important things to think about.

THE SURPRISE

Having become used to having a car I wondered how I was going to get around in this intriguing area without one. Very few people could drive in those days but after only a few days I was introduced to two (who at my age appeared to be) elderly ladies who ran the post office in Torquay. They had a Standard drop-head car in brand new condition and oddly enough did not drive. They were apparently pleased that I was one of the few who had learned to drive and asked me if I would be kind enough to drive them to different places when I had the time free. I enjoyed driving the ladies wherever they wanted to go and fell in love with the surrounding area of Devon that they asked me to drive to. During one such drive I found it slightly embarrassing when an airman saluted me as we drove by. Well, we all make mistakes, but I was chuffed that anyone could mistake me for an officer; it did make me feel that I had perhaps smartened my appearance up a bit.

With the problem of occasional transportation solved, the next question was how to be able to pass inspection and be able to leave the hotel early enough in the evening to enjoy Torquay Bay and its pleasures. The difficulty was that before an airman could leave the hotel he had to pass a uniform inspection; by the time the airman had returned to his room many times for reasons ranging from his buttons not being polished well enough to the way his boots were tied, it meant that by the time your uniform was considered satisfactory it was usually too late to leave the hotel anyway. A uniform inspection was also held every morning. Lined up for the inspection one morning, I was standing at attention next to an old man of thirty by the name of Hamilton who was commended on the mirror shine of his boots. I was admonished for not having my boots polished so well. I realised that doing someone a favour can backfire – I had polished Hamilton's boots for him! I discovered that you could steal out of the hotel over the garage roof (I was tipped off by an officer, believe it or not) and, better still, be able to return as late as you wished by sneaking back in using the same route over the garage roof. Tempting, but I did not use it.

Our holiday in Torquay was spoiled by a very unpleasant corporal who marched large formations of trainees around Torquay at 'double time'. He said he had joined the Air Force in the 1930s because he couldn't get a job and now was enjoying taking it out on these high-born b*****ds. It did annoy me, but I avoided most of his unpleasantness. I had long ago learned how to avoid marches by dodging the head count. I felt justified in avoiding the marches as I did not consider myself a member of the country's elite for whom he apparently held such distaste anyway!

After countless lectures on such subjects as navigation, KRs & ACIs (King's Regulations and Air Council Instructions) which added up to air force law, together with Morse code, etc., etc., etc., it transpired that we apparently were now considered to be capable of being trained as members of an aircrew, although the talk given describing how to side-slip an aircraft with an engine on fire did not fill us with an irresistible desire to jump into an aircraft and experience it for ourselves. Besides what sort of aircraft was he talking about? Aircraft of the First World War? If the German intelligence had become aware of these events, the enemy would have lost the war; they would have all died laughing. But bringing training methods up to meet the requirements of the Second World War would take time. All things considered, what with having the use of the Standard car and enjoying the walks to the 'Drum' at Cockington in the evening, provided a comforting escape from wondering about our unknown future. The Drum (a high-class public house designed by Sir Edwin Lutyens in the 1930s) is nestled in a hard to find hollow in Torquay and is accessible by shady narrow country lanes. The stroll back to the Grand Hotel was fun; we would sing various ditties including one that was sung to the tune of 'She'll be coming round the mountain when she comes', which partly went as follows:

> They'll be flying in formation when they come,
> They'll be flying in formation when they come,
> They'll be flying in formation,
> All the Gerries in creation,
> They'll be flying in formation when they come.

> There'll be six or seven Spitfires in the sky,
> There'll be six or seven Spitfires in the sky,
> Six or seven Spitfires, six or seven Spitfires, six or seven
> Spitfires in the sky.

> Oh, we'll shoot them down in thousands when they come,
> Oh, we'll shoot them down in thousands when they come,
> We'll shoot them down in thousands,
> We'll shoot them down in thousands,
> Yes, we'll shoot them down in thousands when they come.

I suppose we did display a little unearned bravado, something we might have to earn later – hopefully, much later. Although the bravado became more pronounced by the sight of a Royal Air Force officer at the Grand Hotel wearing the American Eagle Squadron insignia patch on the shoulder of his uniform, we were impressed to see one of these much-publicised American airmen.

The trainees were in high spirits and anxious to make progress in their training as was reflected in their impatient chant intoned on a well-known Christmas Carol:

> Oh, why are we waiting?
> Oh, why are we waiting?
> Why are we waiting?
> Oh why, oh why?

The mood was enthusiastic and, if nothing else, the ITW trainees did not seem to contain as many bad apples as at Catterick. I sometimes wondered what had happened to them; they were different from these men who showed the right spirit and were a credit to the country, but how did I get mixed up with them and what happens next? Don't they know my name isn't Superman?

Two weeks' leave was given, together with promotion to LAC (leading aircraftman) and a raise in pay together with the designation 'Aircrew in Training' now being official. Wearing the white flash in my forage cap gave me the feeling that avoiding conscription into the Army by volunteering for the RAF had been the right choice. But I had failed the aircrew selection board twice! Perhaps the board recommendations had been ignored and I now secretly, and perhaps mistakenly, hoped if it were an error, such would not be discovered while I was having such a good time! But what kind of aircrew training did they have in mind for us? The level of instruction taught to us seemed unnecessary for air gunners which left us wondering what were they intending to train us as? Air gunner/radio operators – possibly, but as navigators or pilots, not a chance; but which?

Chapter 3

The Flying Club

I suppose most everyone at one time or another might dream of being able to fly an aeroplane, but if the dream turns into reality, well, flying an aeroplane in wartime might not be such an enticing dream; it was dangerous. Although the thought of flying was entrancing to me, I really did not want to be mistaken for a gung-ho hero, just recognised that I really am not Superman and am just a boy trying to measure up to the risks that wartime flying might involve; but we had been issued with the flying clothing needed for aircrew duties and whether I liked it or not I was probably destined for a posting to an Air Gunner/Radio Operator course, wondering if this was the RAF's equivalent of the Army's 'over the top' in the trenches.

Although I enjoyed the appearance of approval while on leave for my seeming patriotism (you could fool some of the people some of the time), when my leave was over I rejoined the graduates from ITW who were anticipating what their assignments would be. Although not knowing what kind of course I would be assigned, I hoped my rejection for aircrew duties would catch up with me before it perhaps became dangerous. On a Great Western Railway train travelling from Newton Abbot towards London a rumour got around that we were being posted to No. 21 EFTS (Elementary Flying Training School) near Marlow, Buckinghamshire. The rumour turned out to be true and, after arriving at Marlow on the single-coach train from Bourne End, we were driven to the aerodrome located where the road to High Wycombe branched off from the one to Lane End. The countryside was beautiful, and the flying school was on a field that until a few weeks before had been just that, a farmer's field, it had little to show that it was now a 'flying field', other than the DH82a Tiger Moth aeroplanes sitting there waiting. The de Havilland Tiger Moth, a two-wing open-cockpit two-seater aeroplane was designed about 1931 and equipped with a 125hp de Havilland Gypsy Major engine but, except for the Tiger Moths, a hangar and a few huts, No. 21 EFTS might have gone unnoticed behind the tall hedges as it looked like what it was, just a big meadow. The location was idyllic and had the advantage of being within walking distance of Marlow, a delightful Thames Valley town. At this point it seemed they were intending to try to teach me to fly an aeroplane, something I had always dreamed about and I was torn between the desire to continue and take advantage of my dream coming true or be a coward and tell them I really was not Superman and was afraid of what it might entail in the future.

Our arrival was informal and we were assigned to a barrack hut on the opposite side of the road to High Wycombe from the airfield. This posting left me awestruck; the impossible had happened. I was one of twenty *ab-initio* trainees, and they really were intending to try to teach me to become a pilot. This new status provided respect for us that we had not experienced before; even the warrant officer who had formerly been a disciplinarian at a regular RAF base was instructed that the men were not to be marched and would wear shoes instead of the regulation boots. Shoes had been issued to help get the feel of the aircraft's rudder pedals when flying. A flying school? Perhaps I am dreaming; I am just a boy, but is this the dream I have always had coming true?

But back to reality. As any enlisted man in the service knows, he is responsible for maintaining his barrack hut, making up his cot, and keeping everything in accordance with tight military standards, even polishing the heating stove with blacking, and we were enlisted men. But here there was no domestic night (the night each week normally reserved for cleaning the barrack hut at a regular RAF station); for a shilling a week from each of us a lady from the village took care of all these chores and with the promotion to leading aircraftman together with the accompanying raise in pay this was a cheap price to pay. The change to this comparative luxury lacked only one thing, a batman to polish our shoes.

This was not exactly what I had expected when I volunteered for the Royal Air Force; it was perhaps not the nice safe job that I had anticipated, but without doubt it was certainly better than anything that I could have envisioned as a private in the Army. Of course, there was a problem – I had not anticipated getting this close to getting into an aeroplane, although it was exciting to have been issued a Sidcot flying suit, gloves, shoes, helmet, goggles etc. and all the other gear associated with flying in an aeroplane, but we did not have parachutes. The next day that shortcoming was corrected when we were issued with parachutes, together with a lecture and demonstration on how to pack one. I thought it was nice to know how to pack a parachute, but if it does not work on the way down it wouldn't seem to matter. The parachute issued to me was already packed and I could only hope that it had been packed correctly just in case I should have to use it for the purpose it was intended. However, we were assured that if it didn't work they would replace it with another.

But getting this close to an aeroplane let alone to fly in one was enthralling and almost erased my fears (but not quite).

Would flying be fun and turn out to be an exhilarating experience and provide the wonderful feeling of breaking the bonds of earth and the freedom of being able to roam the sky, or would it give a precarious feeling of fear at being high above the ground? Whichever way, if learning to fly at an elementary flying school turned out to be fun, it was still the precursor of the main event, which might be more difficult to describe as fun.

B Flight, to which I was assigned, was located off the road to Lane End, just a short walk from our quarters. At the flight dispersal a few Tiger Moths sat on the grass waiting to be flown. Although apprehensive (alright! Scared) I tried to look inconspicuous, hoping not to be noticed, but an instructor by the name of – oh I know you are not going to believe this, but it is true – Sergeant Flight introduced himself and said, 'get into my aeroplane we are going for a familiarisation flight.' (See plate 2)

I wondered if I had been lulled into a fool's paradise by going with the flow and failing to provide myself with a way out if I was unable to cope. Why had the 'mistake' of my failing aircrew selection interviews been overlooked? I suppose I was both frightened and thrilled to actually come face to face with getting into a real aeroplane. With some trepidation I climbed into the rear open cockpit of the aeroplane and Sergeant Flight climbed into the front one. With the parachute and Sutton harnesses fastened and the Gosport tube (for communication between the pilot and the trainee) connected, Sergeant Flight signalled the mechanic to prop the engine (no self-starter on those aeroplanes), flipped on the ignition switches and the engine started. With that, any last regrets disappeared. The instructor taxied the aeroplane to the take-off point and performed the engine run up (checking the magnetoes and making sure that the engine will not fail on take off). Being satisfied that everything was in order for flight, Sergeant Flight opened the throttle and the aircraft moved forward, gently bouncing as it gained speed and the ground slowly fell away. To my surprise, I found that I was not in the least bit scared and found it to be a very pleasant experience, but that was about to change. The instructor called through the Gosport tube and asked, 'Is your Sutton harness tight?' I replied 'Yes'. There my reverie ended as the pilot performed a slow roll during which, when in the inverted position, I found myself hanging from the aircraft restrained from falling to the ground 4,000 feet below only by my Sutton harness. The instructor followed this manoeuvre by performing a couple of flick rolls and a few loops. At least I think that is what they were since I could not get my head up against the G force to look; the instructor apparently had had his morning fun and returned to the aerodrome and landed.

Strangely, after resuming normal flight any fear that I might have had disappeared. After landing, when asked by the other students about the flight, I responded by saying that it was fine. This apparently was the wrong reply and the others chided me with such remarks as 'oh you probably will be claiming that he did aerobatics and loops'. It did seem prudent not to respond to that, but it did leave me with a slight feeling of superiority, seeing as how I had cheated death in such a display of aerobatics, while all the other students had merely flown around in a manner best suited to little old ladies out for a stroll on a Sunday afternoon.

Having survived this first flight without it leaving any scars either physical or emotional, I thought it might be fun to take advantage of this flying club because it looked like it could be, well, fun – and – get paid for doing it! A pilot's logbook was issued, and a pretty girl named Beatrice was charged with making the appropriate flight-time entries for each of the trainees. I didn't need a plane to fly; I was already in heaven, little realising that this could lead to a place more like hell than heaven.

No. 21 EFTS had only recently been activated and ours was only the second course to be held there; the aeroplanes were all new and maintained by a civilian company by the name of Airwork Ltd. Two of their employees were taxiing aeroplanes, one to the hangar and the other back to the B Flight dispersal but did not allow enough space to pass each other; although no one was hurt I did wonder if they would lose their status of being in a reserved occupation.

Serious flight training began, and the ten exercises required to be accomplished before a student could make his first solo flight started. These exercises comprised, among others, primary and secondary effects of controls, straight and level flight, climbing, gliding and spinning. Except for spinning, the scariest experience I had was when, instead of Sergeant Flight, an officer gave me flying instruction. Until then I had lived in awe of officers and considered them to be some kind of gods who had the ability to cast your soul to purgatory or worse at their slightest whim. However, on my fourth flight an officer holding the rank of flight lieutenant gave me instruction and surprised me by speaking to me as though I was an equal rather than as an officer to an enlisted man. Although this lent a feeling of informality, students always addressed the instructors as 'Sir', regardless of rank, commissioned or otherwise.

I was becoming aware that aircrews had a tendency to informality and conducted themselves as equals when performing their duties as aircrews in flight; each depended upon the others to perform their special skills to ensure the safety of the aircraft regardless of their rank. It was not uncommon for bomber crews to have a sergeant as the captain of the aircraft and another member of the crew to be of commissioned rank, but all members would call the captain 'skipper', regardless of his rank.

I was pleasantly surprised to find that I enjoyed flying although I had a problem; no one, not even myself, knew that I had poor, if any, depth perception. In the air this was not a problem, but the result of not being able to judge my height off the ground when landing caused my 'touchdowns' to be something that left a great deal to be desired. However, the landings probably provided a humorous spectacle of how to make several landings off one approach, but at least after the last bounce the aeroplane always stayed on the ground, making it technically a perfect landing since neither the aeroplane nor its occupants were damaged. The less than desirable landings did not go unnoticed and, after most of the other students had soloed, I had visions of failing and being transferred out of the flying club and so plucked up the courage to ask the flight commander when I would get a solo check ride (wondering if I should have asked 'if', rather than 'when'). The flight commander was perhaps unaware of my less than desirable arrivals which had possibly delayed a solo check ride. I may also have exceeded the number of hours allowed to solo before being suspended but, regardless of any other considerations, he told me to get into his aeroplane. After starting the engine and taxiing out, I completed the vital actions for the before-take-off checklist and saw the petrol cut-off control being pulled back by the instructor. I calmly turned the cut-off back on and opened the throttle for take off; after making three take offs and landings with the gods smiling on me (and, to my surprise each of the landings were perfect), the instructor said 'you stretched the glide a bit on the last one, do one more circuit'. I got lucky again and somehow made a perfect touchdown. Returning to the flight line the instructor got out of the aeroplane and told me to do one circuit on my own. I could hardly believe my ears. I promptly taxied out and took off; over Lane End I waggled my wings with delight at not having an instructor in the front cockpit – I was elated at being alone in the air. My impossible childhood dream had become a reality; I was free of the ground and piloting an aeroplane. Once again I landed and taxied in and lined up my aircraft with the other Tiger Moths on the flight line but, before I got out of the cockpit, my instructor, Sergeant Flight, had returned and walked over to my aircraft and asked 'what have you been up to?' I answered, 'I was sent solo Sir.' I felt sure I was in for a dressing down as he had not sent me for the solo check ride, but instead he told me, 'in that case you had better go and do three more circuits,' so all's well that ends well, and I felt wonderful. But I thought to myself, this is so good; I hope that they never find out about my having failed the aircrew selection board.

Wow, what a day. I was so excited I had failed to realise that the check ride had not been entered in my pilot's logbook, so it could have looked as though I had gone solo without a check ride, but the appropriate check-ride entry was made in my logbook afterwards. After discussing the feelings that the others had about their first solo, without exception they stated that they were apprehensive at being alone in flight without an instructor, so it appears that perhaps I was not bright enough to be scared; I was elated to fly solo.

I suppose I had become an aviator (sounds great, doesn't it?) with no thought as to what the consequences might be when flying is so much fun. I must have started to lose my grip on reality by exposing myself to possible consequences that could result in a day of reckoning, but at that moment I just enjoyed the hard to believe truth that my childhood dream had actually come true and I was able to pilot an aeroplane solo. I felt I had made progress from being a doubtful character to being a little like the Tiger Moth pilot I had once seen who had landed in a field near Five Points when I was on my way home to Leicester from Coventry.

I had permission to have my car at Booker and on a weekend pass drove home to Leicester with three other student pilots whom I dropped off in Northampton near their homes. On the return trip to Booker I picked up my three travelling companions with adequate time to arrive back at the flying school by the 8:00am deadline on Monday, but the car had two flat tyres. I overcame the problem but our time of arrival was delayed until 8:30, resulting in our being put on a charge. My character must have slipped when I told the hearing officer that I was entirely to blame and that the others were helpless in this matter and, as it was not their fault they should not be punished. The hearing officer told me as punishment that I would forfeit a day's pay; apparently the other three received no punishment and I was never aware of a day's pay being deducted either.

With increasing ability to pilot an aeroplane, any flaw in my character did not prevent me from entering into some practices that might have been frowned upon by my superiors, such as challenging other pilots to mock duels at 4,000 feet over the weir at Marlow, or entering into unauthorised aerobatics, although I did obey the rules and performed these manoeuvres in the authorised aerobatics area near Aylesbury. Flying around the High Wycombe area was fun at 1,000 feet and, at that altitude, I found many interesting curiosities, such as a large ball on a steeple in a graveyard. I was told it had been used by the 'Hellfire Club' as a place where they played cards sometime back in the previous century; it seemed to me that they could have found a more pleasant and accessible place than that.

While performing aerobatics in the authorised area I started a manoeuvre at 4,000 feet (aerobatics were to be commenced at an altitude of not less that 4,000 feet above ground level and concluded at an altitude of not less than 3,000 feet). As I lost altitude in the manoeuvre and being less than bright I ended up inside a layer of cloud. Since the Tiger Moth did not have blind-flying instruments, such as an artificial horizon, the only instruments available were an airspeed indicator, a turn-and-bank indicator, an altimeter and a compass. At this point it was too late to wish that I had not entered into aerobatics over the clouds. Realising that a bright spot in the cloud was caused by the sun I was smart enough to know it was supposed to be above me and not off to one side and, with a skill that I did not know I had, I righted the aeroplane and climbed out of cloud, using the turn-and-bank indicator, together with the airspeed indicator. I thought, wow, I had actually flown an aircraft on instruments! Apart from being lucky, it did inspire more confidence in instrument flying, as primitive as they were in a Tigerschmitt, as the Tiger Moth became affectionately called (the name was a touch of bravado and coined from the dreaded German fighter, the Messerschmitt Bf 109). But, although I could cope with a Tiger Moth, I still thought they must be very short of potential pilots for me to be in an aeroplane, and solo at that, but perhaps I was not as bad as I was said to be and perhaps I had not belonged among those ex-cons at Catterick.

One of the heart-stopping exercises required was to restart the engine in flight which was done by first stopping the propeller from rotating by throttling the engine back, switching the magnetoes off and entering into a steep climb until the propeller stopped rotating; with no self-starter it was necessary to point the aircraft straight down until the propeller started to rotate again, then flip the magneto switches back on, open the throttle and bring the aircraft back to level flight. It worked, but the procedure was somewhat 'daunting', to say the least. But sheer terror was experienced when an instructor demonstrated an inverted spin. If you think that being in an aeroplane at 4,000 feet, spinning upside down and even though secured by your Sutton harness you feel that you are being torn out of a corner of the cockpit and thrown at the ground below is not terrifying, just close your eyes and try to imagine it!

With increasing experience piloting the Tiger Moth, I was finding flying to be wonderful and the fun I had imagined it to be; the Moth's inherent desirable characteristics were many, from its low landing speed to the built-in head wind (referring to the drag created by the struts and wires) which pleasantly limited it from building much speed in a dive. Some of its features might even have been considered quaint, from the little spring-loaded flap with an indicator on a left-hand strut acting as an airspeed indicator, although the airspeed indicator in the cockpit was the one actually used in flight. The 'braking' system was fundamental; all it comprised of was a flat metal skid mounted under the tail and used drag to control the speed of the aircraft on the ground, but it did tend to restrict the machine to grass aerodromes. But the pleasure of opening the throttle of a Tiger Moth, lifting the tail for take off and having the wonderful feeling as the aeroplane gathered speed and left the ground caused an addiction to flying that could never be erased. The fun of flying with the little cockpit side flaps down and waving to men fishing on the upper Thames river captivated me in the wonder of being able to fly. The thrill of putting the nose down and applying full throttle to increase the speed to 130 mph, then easing the control column back to perform a loop was exhilarating, although getting a spray of petrol in the face from the fuel tank at the top of the loop did tend to detract from the satisfaction of completing a perfect loop. But by contrast the inverted spin with the feeling of being torn out of a corner of the cockpit was scary; straightening out and turning the aircraft back the right way up felt more like a reprieve than a relief.

Flying the Tigerschmitt was so much fun it titivated my appetite to fly other aeroplanes, especially after seeing other training aircraft, such as the Miles Magister monoplane, affectionately known as the Maggie, which was also used as an *ab-initio* trainer at some of the other elementary flying training schools; additionally a cute-looking little two-seat Cygnet aeroplane visiting Booker looked inviting to fly. My flight time was increasing steadily and I continued to satisfy the requirements laid out in the Royal Air Force *Manual of Elementary Flying Training*, which included dual cross-country exercises, and finding and making approaches to suitable landing sites when the instructor, without warning closed the throttle (although the approach would be discontinued before an actual touchdown it did teach the student pilot to always keep an eye open for suitable landing spots for emergency landings). The cross-country exercises culminated in a solo cross-country flight. I found it enjoyable to fly an aeroplane from one place to another for the first time, instead of landing back at the same aerodrome from which I had taken off.

With the increasing hours of flying the Tiger Moth DH82a, I visited other elementary training aerodromes including one at Bray near Windsor Castle, where I learned the sonnet 'And I'll be the Vicar of Bray', and to satisfy the devil in me I bounced my wheels on the roof of a Great Western Railway passenger train as it sped along the railway lines near Reading. Becoming more daring, I buzzed the army barracks at Aldershot, so low the chimneys were higher than I was; however it did seem that fate smiled upon me as none of these nefarious incidents caught up with me.

The only thing that provided any discord at Booker was the yellow-coloured liver that was served for breakfast one morning – I have loathed liver ever since. So, I did without eating for a few hours and got on with enjoying flying. My mother had knitted a long scarf for me (a very long scarf) to keep me warm in the cold draught of an open cockpit aeroplane and I had fun letting it trail in the slipstream, but it was a nuisance when it got caught on the vertical stabiliser and I let another student borrow it. I wondered what happened to it as LAC Jeavons who borrowed the scarf took it with him to Canada on the Empire Air Training Scheme; he would certainly have had a greater need for it in the far colder climate of the western part of the Canadian prairies than I would in England. But Jeavons could have asked permission to 'borrow' it permanently; not that I would have given it away after my mother had spent so much time and trouble knitting it for me.

The summer weeks passed and the new pilots gained flying time and, hopefully, skills. The autumn was drawing closer and those who had successfully finished the course would be faced with a new and different challenge – the terrors of advanced flying school. I passed the elementary flying school course and was pleasantly surprised that my flying skills had been assessed as 'average'. I had turned a blind eye to the fact that there would be increasing danger in the future after graduating from No. 21 Elementary Flying Training School. But, for now, all was well although it did seem that they were poking fun at my instructor, Sergeant Flight, when they promoted him to the next higher rank and he became Flight Sergeant Flight.

When hearing that the next posting would be to an advanced flying school I made the comment 'oh well, we all have our cross to bear', not realising that it could be a cross, and not necessarily one to bear. However, at that point two weeks' leave was more important than concern about the future, so it was time to enjoy leave in Leicester and, by a coincidence that was to happen many times in the future, both my two friends were also on leave. Sid Johnson, who had sat next to me in school where we were seated at our desks in alphabetical order, was being trained as a glider pilot, attached to the Army's 6th Airborne Division, and Tony Scott, on leave from the Merchant Navy, was being trained to become a ship's officer. The three of us became known as the 'Three Caballeros' after the characters in a Walt Disney film. The carefree behaviour of the three of us belied the fact that there was a war going on around us.

Although I was still just a boy we Three Caballeros were now eighteen years of age and, although we enjoyed an occasional beer, we did not smoke. Our natural exuberance and carefree antics did not go unnoticed, although at the time it was probably a comic relief to observers and a diversion from the realities of war. One of our antics was for one of us to stand on a concrete-and-brick structure that shielded some ground-level windows of buildings from bomb blasts and deliver a sermon on 'The Evils of Drink'. Being in uniform, this invariably drew a small crowd of amused observers and, while the preacher was invoking laughs from the crowd, the other two would pass the hat around. This operation was continued until enough small change had accumulated to buy a round of drinks and the three of us would then retreat merrily into the nearest pub, usually the Rainbow and Dove on Charles Street and which we always referred to as the 'Rook and Flarepath'. Although the pay we received was meagre it did seem rather a subversive way of collecting a few pennies, but everyone enjoyed our absurd behaviour. They also seemed to enjoy the spectacle of the three of us after a drink, wandering down the street arm in arm singing 'We Three Caballeros, we gay Caballeros, they say we are Birds of a Feather', which, of course, was also borrowed from the Walt Disney film. But all good things come to an end, Sid went back to 6th Airborne Division, Tony to his Anglo-American oil tanker and I to my new, although temporary, posting to another farmer's field now being used by the RAF, this station's name being RAF Station Clyffe Pypard.

Clyffe Pypard was nothing more than a grass field with a solitary hangar, situated at the top of a sharp escarpment overlooking Swindon. The only duties required of the newly trained but inexperienced pilots were to terrify the local people living at the bottom of the escarpment by taking off in their brand-new Tiger Moths and diving down the escarpment, disturbing the local residents drinking their afternoon tea. Because the student pilots were merely on standby until courses at advanced flying schools became available, the time at Clyffe Pypard was limited, but it was a wonderful experience to fly over the Vale of Evesham towards the Bristol Channel and enjoy the pleasant English countryside. Life was good and being paid for the pleasure of flying added frosting to the cake. Later, Sid Johnson would also enjoy flying at Cliffe Pypard as he progressed in his training as a glider pilot.

Chapter 4

This is Serious

WARNING

If you are not afraid of flying, you might be after reading this.

The carefree flying club atmosphere of the elementary flying school was quickly dispelled by the next course; you soon became aware that you were expected to mature from a boy with a toy aeroplane to Superman or die in the process, and many did.

Advanced flying school is where an attempt is made to transform light aeroplane drivers into combat pilots. The effort was made at No. 5 SFTS (Service Flying Training School), Ternhill, in Shropshire, but changing boys flying toy aeroplanes into men flying modern fighter aircraft was a task fraught with danger (and deaths). RAF Station Ternhill was a pre-war grass aerodrome; it had grim two-storey brick barrack blocks, a parade ground and guards on duty at the entrance gate. It was a forbidding place in contrast to the carefree ambience of an elementary flying school. The atmosphere was not enhanced by the war having visited one of the pre-war hangars where a Luftwaffe bomb had blown a large part of the roof away; it was jokingly referred to as 'the sunshine hangar'. We were assigned quarters in one of the two-storey brick barracks with little knowledge of what lay ahead and went through the usual sign-in routine and collecting our ritual tea mugs.

A greeting was provided in the station theatre by an RAF officer who 'welcomed' us to No. 5 SFTS, warning us that unauthorised flying practices would not be tolerated and, to make his point clear, told us that 'two trainees had engaged in unauthorised formation flying the day before and made a fighter-boy peel-off'; 'they are being buried tomorrow'; end of welcome! (See plate 1)

This sombre greeting did not create a gung-ho feeling that we 'might' become Royal Air Force pilots; it was more like 'if'! We were somewhat less than relaxed now that we were being introduced to this new kind of 'flying club'. It was obvious that the atmosphere we had been accustomed to at elementary flying school and Cliffe Pypard was not one that we would have here. It was too late to tell them that I had failed the aircrew selection board as the result had obviously been ignored and I was stuck with this apparently more dangerous stage of flight training. Knowing I probably would not be able to cope with flying advanced aircraft due to my landing difficulties did blunt any optimism that I might have had, but I decided I would give it my best shot. The future appeared a little more tolerable knowing that I would probably be identified as an unsatisfactory student and suspended anyway. There were officers on the course, and I, as an enlisted airman with the lowly rank of leading aircraftman, would be left at the starting gate; any flying shortcomings that I might have would be less likely to be overlooked and result in my being suspended anyway, so a slight (very slight) cheerfulness set in as the threat of a sudden demise was somewhat reduced. It did cross my mind that if I was suspended I would probably be transferred to far less stressful duties such as sweeping out hangars etc.; after all I would not be much of a loss, all that I had done until now was to learn how to fly a light aeroplane and I would still be able to boast that I had been taught to be a pilot (if only somewhat). However, the tantalising thought lingered that I might possibly someday become a competent Royal Air Force pilot (see what comes of watching too many moving pictures?). I suppose I harboured a faint hope that I might be able to cope with the challenge of advanced flying and perhaps be able to imitate one of those dashing RAF pilots. In that frame of mind I figured that I had better test the waters, but the danger was still there. Although it seemed to bother me less, I was more concerned about what my relatives might fear for my safety, but I supposed those were the thoughts that the other trainees had too.

About fifty student pilots were enrolled in the course, which included the officers from other services (the officers would be transferred to the Royal Air Force upon successful completion of pilot training). Though mostly British, some trainees came from other parts of the world, but most were from the British Commonwealth. It was quite a mix: there were Australians, Jamaicans (both black and white), a few from the Indian sub-continent, South Africa, one from the Seychelles, and even one from China (his family had moved to England from Hong Kong at the start of the war). Also included were six members of the French *Armée de l'air* who had escaped across the English Channel from their homeland, now occupied by the Germans. One student pilot's father had fought in the Great War – on the German side – but the family had become disillusioned by the National Socialist party headed by Adolf Hitler and left for Britain in 1934.

Not unexpectedly, nicknames were quickly attached as trying to remember the real names of so many was a challenge. However, I was not impressed by the nickname that was bestowed on me; somehow I was not able to reconcile the change of my nickname from Snake-hips to 'Bonzo the Negro' (the name was probably derived from Ken 'Snake-hips' Johnson being black), although at that time no one had any thoughts about where a person came from or whether they were black, yellow, white, olive or some other tint of the rainbow; there were more pressing things occupying our minds.

The nearest town was Market Drayton, several miles away from Ternhill and too far to walk; so the pub across the road from the main gate created a diversion for some of the men although the 'Stormy Petrel', colloquially known as the 'Mucky Duck', did not hold any interest for me. The sectioned aeroplane engines displayed at Ternhill were of more interest and I spent a great deal of time studying the engines, together with the mock-up of the Hawker Hurricane fighter cockpit. I thought the more unpleasant aspects of the introduction into service life were now over and such things as visits to the dentist's torture chamber had ended, I was unpleasantly brought back to reality when ordered to report for a dental examination which, of course, resulted in my being subjected to further dental treatment. The treatment involved several visits over a period of time and imvolved many fillings and other dental tortures. Aircrew members, naturally, needed their teeth to be in perfect condition to avoid dental pain while flying, although it did provide a little false comfort that they would not go to all this trouble if they expected you to have an early demise; any kind of optimism was better than none at all. Although having healthy teeth was important, it did not make the treatment less painful by knowing that; however one of the fillings occasionally created a sudden sharp pain, especially when eating, but the occasional stabbing pain was preferable to a return visit to the dentist's torture chamber.

My introduction to flying in an advanced trainer was made with a mixture of curiosity and apprehension. The apprehension was not diminished when I was ordered to get into the front cockpit of a Miles Master that seemed to be an enormous aeroplane in comparison to a Tiger Moth. (See plate 3)

Wearing my Sidcot flying suit, flying boots, leather gloves, leather helmet and goggles, I did give the appearance of being an aviator, but I certainly did not feel like one. After climbing into the cockpit I was neither curious nor apprehensive. I think the correct expression is scared stiff. After buckling my parachute and the Sutton harness and connecting the Gosport tube, the instructor in the rear cockpit told me to adjust my seat height and move the rudder pedals to a position where I would be able to operate the controls. This aircraft, a Miles Master Mk 2, was equipped with a Pratt and Whitney radial engine and had a full blind-flying instrument panel in addition to many other instruments. I wondered how anyone could comprehend, let alone know what they were for or how to use them. This made me think that failing this course, whether I tried or not, was inevitable. My instructor, a stern flight sergeant, gave a signal to the ground crew to start winding a crank at the back of the engine. It created a whining noise that increased in intensity until the handle was removed. The instructor then engaged the inertial starter (a type fitted to many American engines) and the engine roared into life. It seemed to be such a huge engine and the three-blade propeller looked enormous in comparison to the tiny two-blade propeller of the Tiger Moth. The summation of all the things that were happening numbed me to the point of not really grasping that I was about to be launched into the air in this big, heavy, advanced trainer. After the instructor waved the chocks away he taxied the machine to the take-off position and performed the 'vital actions' before take off; the instructor told me through the Gosport tube to make sure my harness was tight.

I was not prepared for the violent acceleration that the powerful Pratt and Whitney Wasp engine provided; it roared down the airfield and, although the aircraft quickly became airborne, it was in a far more authoritative manner than the gentle flutter into the air of a Tiger Moth. The unexpected loud shrieking noise after take off made by the undercarriage being retracted for a moment added to my fright. There were so many confusing instruments in the cockpit such as the gyro-compass that I had been instructed to uncage after the engine was started and, although I tried to remember, the instructions on how and what they were used for were lost on me in this moment of near panic; even conscription into the Army looked a lot less formidable in comparison. Thankfully, this was only a familiarisation flight and there were no points to be made and after the frightening experience of the undercarriage being lowered and the flaps extended, the aeroplane threw itself at the ground like a lift gone berserk; it was a relief when the plane touched down smoothly on the grass. After the instructor had taxied to the hard standing and switched the engine off, he asked, 'How did you like it?' Being afraid of giving the wrong answer, I lied when I replied, 'very good sir'. I did not want the instructor to know it had scared the living daylights out of me. I was instructed to get the Miles Master operating handbook and learn by heart the walk-round inspection procedure for the aircraft, 'the vital actions before engine start', the 'vital actions before take off', the 'vital actions after take off', the 'vital actions before landing' and the 'vital actions after landing'. Learning how to read is one thing, but reading and memorising all this information in just a few hours and being able to remember it is something else, how would I be able to remember all of these things, let alone be able to accomplish them knowing there was no room for error. I did not sleep well that night.

From the operating manual I learned that there were three different models of the Miles Master, the main difference being the type of engines with which they were fitted, and that the aircraft was constructed of wood due to the shortage of metal fabrication materials which were needed for the manufacture of combat aircraft. Reading the flight manual also made me aware of the many innovations in the design of the aircraft; being of a mechanical bent I was impressed by the grouping of the engine controls together with the other innovative features which included tubular push-pull control connections of the flight-control surfaces instead of the more common method of connecting them with wires. Although reading the manual did not relieve me of any apprehension, I did my best to memorise as much of the information that I could, but absorbing all the knowledge required to fly such an advanced aircraft in such a short space of time in just a few hours was demanding to say the least. But the arousal of interest in the design of the aircraft made me want to find out more about it and I hoped the knowledge might help overcome some of my feelings of apprehension. Trying to remember all the things that I had been instructed to learn was mindboggling, but I did my best. I wish I could make some funny remarks about the mindnumbing events that were happening, but my sense of humour seemed to have disappeared.

The following morning, I practised the walk-round inspection and even got into the cockpit. Although mentally in a daze, I practised going through all the vital actions just in case I should find myself in a position that I would have to use them. It was perhaps fortunate that I did because I still felt totally lost and in a very confused state at this point; flying a Miles Master after previously flying only a Tiger Moth would be like driving a high-powered racing car after having only ridden a bicycle before. The instructor having observed me accomplish the walk-round inspection correctly, unsmilingly ordered me to climb into the aircraft and make the necessary adjustments to my seat height and the rudder pedals and wait for further instructions.

Since I realised that I had better make a point of familiarising myself with the cockpit instruments in the flight manual, I had studied what they were and what they were used for and they now seemed a little less intimidating. I even found that I would like to see how they worked – I was soon to find out. The instructor secured himself in the rear cockpit and talked me through the engine start procedure; after the engine roared to life I was told to adjust the throttle to idle and go through the procedure of uncaging the artificial horizon and the gyrocompass, although the instructor initiated the taxi. After removal of the chocks he instructed me to taxi to the take-off point but to keep the control column pulled back in order to avoid any tendency for the aircraft to nose over, this being a tail dragger and prone to nosing over when power was applied; tricycle undercarriages were still rare on aircraft at that time. Although much larger than the Tiger Moth, the Magister's nose still restricted straight-ahead vision, making it necessary for the plane to be yawed from side to side with the rudder to see where you were going. On reaching the take-off point I ran the engine up (checking to ensure that the magneto drop was within limits) and checked that the trim tab was correctly set, the variable pitch propeller set in full-fine pitch and that the fuel was turned on and sufficient. These were the vital actions before take off and, together with all the other essential actions, were necessary to ensure that the aircraft would get off the ground safely. The instructor then told me to make sure that no other aircraft would be interfered with and to advance the throttle fully for take off; he must have been tired of living. But there was not much tendency for the aircraft to swing and I was so busy trying to keep the beast under control I forgot to be scared and even remembered to retract the undercarriage after becoming airborne. After closing the canopy, reducing power and RPM (revolutions of the propeller), 'the vital actions after take off' were completed and the aircraft settled into a normal cruise, I found the aircraft handled well and was not difficult to control. The ensuing flight enabled me to understand and be able to use some of the instruments with a reasonable degree of competency, but although trying hard to satisfy the stern instructor he was totally unforgiving of anything less than perfection, which in a perverted way caused me to feel more inadequate. Trying my hardest, I received nothing but criticism with no approval when I might have done anything right; this made me more afraid of the instructor than the aeroplane as anything I did seemed to be wrong and my lack of depth perception didn't help make my landings anything less than dangerous arrivals. Although I was beginning to feel reasonably confident about controlling the aeroplane in flight, when trying to land, the aeroplane knew who was in control – and it was not me. After a few hours of flight time on the Miles Master, trainees were being taken for solo check rides. I was surprised when an officer ordered me into his aircraft for a check ride, I knew I could never solo this aircraft and the result was inevitable – I failed the check ride. It was lunchtime and my instructor was told that I did not accomplish the 'vital actions before take off' correctly and had taken off directly towards No.3 MU (Maintenance Unit), some three miles distant from the aerodrome; I guess he did not bother to add that my landing was more like an accident than a landing. My instructor did not agree with the reasons for failing me because that was the way he had taught me and he considered that taking off toward the MU was correct since that was directly into wind and the MU was far away. Tragically, the officer who had failed me was killed in an accident during the lunchtime break and had not written the failure report. My instructor, feeling that his flying instruction had been impugned, took it upon himself and told me to go solo; I knew I was not ready to solo, although not for the reasons given for failing the solo check flight. I just could not land and was afraid to take the aeroplane up on my own, but I could not disobey the order, so I prepared to commit suicide. Feeling unnerved by the sudden death of the officer I had just flown with, it was with a feeling of trepidation that I started the engine and taxied the aircraft into position for take off. After completing the vital actions before take off, I opened the throttle and committed myself to flight. As I climbed to altitude and flew around the circuit, I looked down at the ground on the downwind leg and, knowing I could not land, said out loud to myself 'but how am I going to get it down?' I made the approach to hit down saying to myself, 'I don't care how much it bounces, once it hits the ground and I've throttled back I am not going to do anything but hold on and hope that the aeroplane will eventually stop bouncing and come to a stop.' It came to pass; after many extraordinary attempts to make holes in the ground the aeroplane came to a stop and, to my surprise, all in one piece. No mention was made of my unusual arrival; either no one was watching or they had covered their eyes. I was pleased that I had managed to make the solo flight despite the spectacle of my landing, but would I have to do it again?

I was afraid of being unable to cope and the fatal crash when the check-ride instructor had been killed was only the first of many fatal crashes. These created a pall over any level of confidence that I might have had after going solo and the solo flight had held none of the pleasure that I had experienced making my first solo in a Tiger Moth at elementary flying school. I felt confused; my object in avoiding conscription into the Army had morphed

31

into a circumstance that I could not have foreseen and I felt at odds that although I was happy to be able to control one of these 'monsters' in the air I was miserable that I could not land it. It appeared that I was not about to be suspended at this stage and, not being able to remain airborne indefinitely after take off, I somehow had to find a way to land safely with or without the help of an instructor, but how? This was a lot different from the childish dream of some day being able to fly one of those slow biplanes; the dream had seemed entrancing and those aeroplanes were made of wood, canvas, string and wire; but now they were built of metal and capable of carrying bombs, machine guns and cannon, and not being able to land one could result in a very limited future.

But winter was approaching and, while trying to walk a straight line across the airfield in a thick fog, out of the gloom a ghostly figure appeared from the opposite direction. It was another airman also lost in the fog; he told me that the Americans had been attacked by the Japanese at Pearl Harbor. Neither of us knew exactly where Pearl Harbor was, except that it was on an island somewhere in the Pacific Ocean. The news of the Japanese forces creating havoc in the Pacific saddened me; the people of America who were only now recovering from the great depression would be dragged into the war. I had the feeling that until now it somehow had been a private war and that was bad enough, but it seemed that the misery of war was spreading across the world. Never mind if they are unable to transform me into Superman I will just have to do my best to try and save the world.

A few days later, in addition to being at war with Japan, the United States of America was also at war with Germany and Italy, when both countries declared war. British territory in Malaya was also attacked by the Japanese; the war was now truly a global conflict. Although the expansion of the war made no noticeable difference to our training, the facilities for pilots were fast becoming overcrowded at Ternhill. Accidents were increasing and most of them were fatal. To alleviate the congestion, training units were transferred on temporary assignment to one of two 'satellite' fields, one at Childs Arcul and the other at Chetwynd, near the town of Newport, Shropshire. We were in B Flight, which was assigned to Chetwynd, which was nothing but a very large farmer's field, bare except for the hut that served as our quarters, a hut to wash in, and a hut from which our activities would be directed. These facilities without fear of contradiction would be considered primitive and a far cry from us being showered with any comfort, but it did have one saving grace; it was within walking distance of the charming town of Newport, Shropshire – a long walk, but worthwhile (see plate 4).

THIS IS SERIOUS

My nineteenth birthday on 5 December was used as the excuse for a party at the Stormy Petrel across the road from the entrance to Ternhill. It was a party that I had difficulty remembering due to being plied with sixteen (according to the report) glasses of wine that caused me to become somewhat incapacitated. Having been introduced to the effects of alcohol and the unpleasant after-effects, I did not imbibe again until one evening in Newport before I attended a dance in the local hall; a young lady (I do not remember her name or even whether she was pretty) taught me to 'dance', an art that I was totally unable to master or perform again unless I had indulged in a sufficient libation of alcoholic drinks.

In the unheated barrack hut at Chetwynd that winter, sleeping, even with the three blankets that were issued, was akin to sleeping in the Arctic without a tent. Despite the blankets, the Arctic might have been considered warm by comparison. To find some respite from the intolerable, I asked for and was given permission to bring the three blankets I had been issued with at Ternhill to the unheated freezer in which we were quartered at Chetwynd. With six blankets, it temporarily warded off the problem of freezing to death until someone felt I had no right to cheat death and stealthily stole all but one of my blankets. With only one blanket I would probably have frozen to death in the frigid weather had not fate intervened and it started to snow heavily. Since the only snow removal equipment consisted of a host of airmen wielding shovels, and there not being any shovels, all flying activities came to a halt. It was decided to send us home on indefinite leave to be recalled when weather conditions permitted flying to resume. I was especially grateful for this decision; it probably saved me from freezing to death. Six weeks later the weather warmed up and the snow melted and I was recalled; my disillusionment in the lack of esprit de corps and concern in looking after each other had appalled me. I had imposed some standards on myself, and felt that I did not want to be part of an aircrew and be in a position of having to rely on people who had demonstrated such a dangerous lack of consideration for others. Because of this, together with being unable to cope with landing, I felt I was a loser and decided to avoid what was beginning to appear to be an untenable position. I decided not to return when ordered.

However, being AWOL (absent without official leave) did not sit well with me and, after two days, I returned to Ternhill to face the music. I had remembered many years before seeing the RAF airship R101 fly overhead and thinking of how wonderful it would be to be able to fly. (The R101 airship, while on a flight to India, crashed in France killing all on

33

board.) That thought had not disillusioned me from flying when I grew up and although the opportunity to fly had occurred in an entirely different way to what I could have imagined, I had developed a sense of duty that spurred me to return, even if the result was a court martial. Realising my stupidity would accomplish nothing, I returned to Ternhill to face the music. The gods must have been smiling on me; either that or they were so short of pilots that they could not afford to lose even one. They decided not to put me on a charge, but I would be informally punished by teaching me a new trade. I was told to spend a day washing windows. The window-washing instruction was informally taught by a friendly sergeant who told me to 'take care of the corners and the middle will take care of itself'. It seemed to work, but to call it punishment would be a misnomer, I was so relieved that cleaning the windows seemed more of a pleasure than a punishment; perhaps George Formby was on to something.

It penetrated my thoughts that, on 3 September 1939 (the day the UK declared war), few people in England could drive and only a handful could fly aeroplanes; anyone with my background being taught to fly was beyond the realm of feasibility, yet here I was doing just that. The only barrier to becoming a competent pilot was that I could not land safely, so I felt I had to find a technique to master the art of landing, with or without help, even if I was killed trying. My lack of ability to land in a satisfactory (safe) manner had not gone unobserved, and when I was told to go and make three circuits and landings I decided there had to be something I could do. I had an idea and tried something different. As I approached for landing, instead of trying to guess my exact height off the ground, I brought the aircraft in as close to the ground as I could judge with power on and in a three-point attitude. I then slowly closed the throttle, letting the aircraft gently sink to the ground; the touchdown was smooth and it seemed so simple that I could hardly believe that it was anything but luck. Encouraged by the result of the first attempt, I made the remaining two approaches using the same technique, each time resulting in perfect three-point landings. I was elated at having solved the problem without help, a problem that had existed since I started flying but, of course, lack of depth perception was not a common condition and instructors would not have had the experience to help anyway. Later by circumstance I had the opportunity to take a glimpse of the progress book and was happy to see the following notation: 'I sent Johnson to make three landings and observed each of them to be perfect.' I felt that I had accomplished the impossible and I was now off the hook.

But I was not off the hook. My early lack of co-ordination had been observed and I was taken on a 'wash-out check ride', the preliminary before being suspended from flight training and it was the last thing I wanted now that I had solved the landing problem and was beginning to feel able to complete the course. The squadron leader conducting the check ride demonstrated a tight turn to the right and, by kicking in hard-left rudder, converted it into a hard turn to the left. After straightening the aircraft out he instructed me to repeat the manoeuvre. Although I tried, I found that in the hazy weather with no visible horizon I failed hopelessly to accomplish the manoeuvre. Knowing this would result in my being suspended, I urgently asked the instructor for permission to try again and, to my own wonderment (and probably that of the instructor), I executed the manoeuvre perfectly. The instructor continued the test and instructed me to pull my hood over, blanking out any outside visual reference, but flying on instruments was easy for me as I had practised instrument flying whenever possible and spent a great deal of time in the link trainer. When told to come out from under the hood I was asked to identify where we were, together with the knowledge of the course I had flown. I observed a small lake beneath and, despite the poor visibility, it was easy to guess Ellesmere Lakes. Of course, I was right and was instructed to take him back to Chetwynd. In the poor visibility and without reference to a map I just took my best guess at the heading; once again I was right, although only instinctively I had ended up on the correct side of the airfield to make the landing approach. I was happy that the instructor took over the aeroplane and landed; a bad landing by me could have spoiled an otherwise very successful day.

Now, no longer threatened with suspension, I felt I was not only growing up, I was becoming able to compete with the others and decided that whatever it took I would finish the course; you can tell my sense of humour was returning. However, the fatal accidents continued to occur; an aircraft crashed into a copse close to the airfield at Chetwynd, killing an Army officer and his warrant officer instructor. The reality of death was gruesomely brought home when someone morbidly had gone to the crash site after the clean-up and found what he thought was a wet sinewy piece of a tree limb, until he realised that there was a wrist watch on it. It was just one of many crashes. A Hawker Hurricane crashed nearby, killing the pilot, one of the instructors, but a mental barrier was erected to counteract these happenings, a necessity in order to carry on; the tragedy was reduced to finding out if there was any of the canopy found. Model aircraft or pilots' wings were made using the Perspex from which the canopy was made; the attitude toward death became callous, but that was war.

Near accidents were not uncommon and I found that I was not immune to them either. Three of the Free French Air Force student pilots flying that day included Marcelle Lorand, an airman named Hardy and a third named Thibodaux, who had volunteered for pilot training after escaping from German-occupied France, one by rowing a boat across the English Channel together with his little sister.

It was normal for many take offs and landings to be made at the same time on this large grass airfield. One of the French pilots had touched down and was on his landing run as I started my take-off run on a parallel course on his right-hand side. As he slowed down he suddenly veered into my path. Having almost reached flying speed I had no place to go and kicked in right rudder and, with just enough air speed, I was able to lift my left wing over the right wing of the French pilot's aircraft and avoid a collision. I continued my take off but had the presence of mind to glance at the other aircraft. I saw the pilot had his head turned away in the opposite direction; that French pilot probably never knew how close to death we both came that day. I vowed never to let anything like that happen again. I must have lost any sense I might have had. With all the people being killed, why did I feel compelled to continue? (See plate 5)

But despite those considerations my skills had improved to the point of being proficient on all three of the Miles Master variants from the Mk 1 with the 650hp Rolls Royce Kestrel engine (the same engine model that Willy Messerschmitt had used to power the prototype of his Bf 109 fighter), the Mk 2 with the Pratt and Whitney Wasp Junior engine and the Mk 3, powered by a Bristol Mercury engine, but flying one at night sounded more like suicide than an exercise. But, like it or not, the aerodrome was prepared for night flying by marking a runway path on the grass field at Ternhill with a row of gooseneck flares to mark the runway and appropriately named the 'flare path'. A controller using an Aldis Lamp authorised take offs – green to authorise take off and red for don't. After two flights around the circuit with an instructor, who observed and encouraged the student to correctly navigate the circuit without becoming disorientated or lost, probably with a sigh of relief he signed off the student as ready to make a night circuit of the field – solo. After I had satisfied my instructor, it was my turn. I started the engine of my aircraft (a Master Mk 2 with the Pratt and Whitney engine) and taxied to the take-off point. After run up and receiving a green light, I opened the throttle and after becoming airborne retracted the undercarriage and started the 180-degree turn onto the downwind leg thinking this is not too bad, but when I looked down for the flare path it was not there. It was above my head. I was upside down. I swear at that point that I felt the boney hand of the grim reaper in my back saying 'I've got you'. However, he got soft and let me regain control. With my self-confidence now reduced to zero, I had learned the hard way always to keep an eye on the blind-flying instruments unless you are tired of living. It was frightening if you lost sight of the flare path as there were no other lights to be seen anywhere in the blackout (Oh, I don't want to think about it). Little did I realise that in the not too distant future I would experience just that problem and have to find an airfield in the pitch-black darkness with neither cockpit lighting, radio nor maps to help me. There were a few more night-flying exercises to be performed that provided a night-flying experience that added a little humour when the fire crew attempted to put out the flames from the exhaust of a Pratt and Whitney engine. It would have been the correct thing to do, except for one thing: the Pratt and Whitney engine normally emitted flames from the exhaust when it was idled. It was a sight worth watching, but everyone, including the fire crew, had to learn. Fortunately it was the only one that they tried to put out.

After many more hours gaining experience my flying skills had improved to the point that I was considered capable of flying a Hawker Hurricane fighter, the aeroplane of the type that had been the mainstay of Fighter Command during the recent Battle of Britain (see plate 6). By sitting in the mock-up cockpit of the Hurricane I had familiarised myself with the layout and operation of the instruments and controls until I was able to touch each of the controls with my eyes closed. I memorised the descriptions of the aircraft handling characteristics, together with approach speeds, undercarriage and flap extension speeds, as well as the engine and RPM settings needed to safely fly the aeroplane. There was no room for error since, it being a single-seat fighter, there could be no check ride – sounds scary doesn't it?

All I had done was join the air force expecting a nice safe unskilled job and was now considered capable of flying a real fighter, but I had the self-confidence and looked forward to flying the Hawker Hurricane. When told to fly it, I did the preliminary checks and walk-round and climbed into the cockpit. With my parachute harness fastened I secured myself in the cockpit with the Sutton harness and adjusted the seat height and rudder pedals. I was now ready to start the Rolls Royce Merlin engine. I enjoyed the low roar of the Merlin engine as I taxied out to the take-off position and, after performing the 'vital actions before take off', turned into wind and opened the throttle. I was elated as the plane broke ground and, after retracting the undercarriage, I throttled back and adjusted the constant-speed propeller to the correct settings for climb and found the aircraft was easy to handle, revelling in the same feeling of elation that I had experienced on my first solo in the Tiger Moth. I made full use of the hour or more I was authorised to fly and felt out the aircraft, performing everything from stalls to imitating fighter tactics, but stayed short of performing aerobatics although I felt at one with the machine. I revelled in the beautifully balanced controls and finished this fascinating flight with a perfect three-point landing using the technique that I had developed with the Miles Master. So, who wants to sweep out hangars? I knew I could not only finish the course, I was becoming an accomplished pilot.

None of the aircraft used for training at Ternhill were fitted with radios except for a few Hurricanes equipped with the standard TR9-D radios. I imagined that a powerful ground transmitter/receiver was used to direct the fighters during the recent Battle of Britain since the range of the radios appeared to be extremely limited. I tried to practise use of the radio while flying a Hurricane. The only way I was able to contact a ground station was by flying directly over it; I figured shouting might have been more effective. This failed to inspire any confidence in the airborne radio communications equipment installed at that time and I could only assume that the fighter pilots who had used them must have been flying in tight formation to communicate with each other and the little clock-like gadget that was supposed to be used with the radio was lost on me. Transmitting was a bit intimidating; it was not like speaking into a telephone. Anyone could listen to a radio transmission; it was like talking on a stage in front of a huge audience and not being able to see them or know who they were. Initially, it did cause me to have a little stage-fright about using such equipment.

I felt that I had become proficient flying a Hurricane and indulged in what I termed a 'rolling cross-country'. I performed 360-degree rolls the entire way around a triangular cross-country flight. On another occasion after a snowstorm, I found my way over the featureless landscape to buzz my sister's house in Groby. It was the first time we had flown with snow covering the landscape. After returning I was asked by other pilots if I had difficulty navigating over the featureless countryside. I replied no, not at all. Sarcastically the remark was made 'I suppose you'll claim you found your way home and buzzed your house.' Well, what could I say? On another flight after doing slow rolls at 7,000 feet over my home in Leicester, I closed the throttle over Swithland Reservoir to lose height and closed the canopy.

This trapped the cuffs of my gauntlets between the canopy and the windscreen. With my hands trapped as if handcuffed, I could only control the aircraft with my knees. If the scene had been in a Keystone Cops film everyone would have laughed, but I did not find it funny. (Oh, I was not killed; I got my hands free, look out Houdini!) But flying was great fun although there were drawbacks; flying a Hurricane without wearing gloves could cause the back of your hands to become very bloody due to the many sharp projections in the cockpit. I learned that the hard way.

The continuing bombing of British cities weighed heavily on my mind; the cities in which I had lived had been bombed and the centre of Coventry had been virtually obliterated. It brings it home to you what war is when streets you used to walk down and the shops where you bought things are reduced to piles of rubble. The scream of falling bombs and the feeling of relief when you realised the bomb blasts had missed and you were still alive after they hit the ground, the violation of things I treasured and the suffering of people in the aftermath of these bombing raids changed my attitude towards avoiding exposure to the 'discomforts' of war. It changed me from just trying to avoid conscription into the Army as a private to feeling determined to end this insanity. With the self-esteem and readiness to do my duty, I was now ready to take an active part in defending my country (did I really say that?). During training I had not faced the reality that I could actually end up facing danger as a combat pilot; the possibility had appeared to be so far in the distance that it had failed to register in my mind, but it did not detract from my newfound joy of being able to fly an actual fighter and I was ready.

Advanced flying training continued, and the number of accidents was reducing the number of students left on the course, but I had adopted the philosophy of convincing myself that it would always be someone else who 'bought the farm'. To relieve congestion at Ternhill and provide the pilots with experience of flying from concrete runways that were now becoming more commonplace, the flight was moved to RAF Station Molesworth in Bedfordshire on temporary assignment. The airfield was still under construction and had long runways designed for heavy bombers; the accommodations, although new, were sparse but adequate. The modern control tower was intriguing; it had controls for a Drem lighting system that provided circuit lights and lead-in funnels to the threshold of the active runway to aid bombers returning to land at night. Of course, the Drem lighting system would not be of use to us, as we would not be flying at night. The sight of inexperienced pilots who had only flown from forgiving grass airfields and who now were trying to learn the technique of landing on hard unforgiving concrete runways was something to behold; fortunately no accidents occurred in this endeavour. The difficulties displayed by some of the other pilots attempting to land on a hard runway gave me a slight feeling of superiority as the method of landing that I had developed yielded a perfect three-point landing for me every time, on either concrete runways or grass.

The time at Molesworth did take on more of an atmosphere of a flying club; good food as opposed to air force food, was available at the canteen that the construction company (Wimpy) had set up for its workers. The luxury of tinned fruit and cakes always available for a good tuck-in made a pleasant break once in a while and was a break from the reality of the war we were preparing for.

Flying activities continued at Molesworth and with no accidents occurring, but there were amusing incidents. A ground mechanic hitched a ride around the airfield by lying across the leading edge of the horizontal stabiliser of a Hurricane, a common practice as it was the position that a mechanic would assume to weigh down the rear of the fuselage to prevent the aircraft nosing over when the engine was run up to full power as accomplished before take off. But, in this case, the pilot turned his aircraft onto the runway and applied power for take off without the check; fortunately the mechanic had no desire to fly and hurriedly removed himself from the tail plane. I bet that airman didn't have a smile on his face afterwards and doubt that he found it amusing.

A little *déjà vu* occurred when I was instructed to do a formation take off and fly in formation with another Miles Master containing an instructor and student. The take-off roll was initiated by the instructor in the other aircraft and, although the initial roll was normal, as they reached flying speed the instructor's aircraft started drifting to the right. With visions of the near miss at Chetwynd with the French pilot, I realised that I was being squeezed to the right of the runway in tight formation. With the right wing of the lead aircraft getting closer, I was forced to move closer to the edge of the unfinished concrete which had a one-foot drop on the side. I had nowhere to go and no room to spare. I reacted in the only way I could and pulled the aircraft off the ground; it staggered into flight with barely enough speed to remain airborne. Wondering what on earth, or in this case, off the earth, was the instructor doing to allow this to happen, I continued to hold the tight formation and stayed in close during some fairly violent manoeuvres but eventually I broke off when it became apparent that neither the instructor nor his student had any idea that I was still in formation. After landing I asked what had happened. The instructor said that he had forgotten that he had instructed me to do a formation take off and was unaware that I was still in formation during the flight. Although he complimented me on my flying abilities, that was of little consolation for what would have happened to me if I had gone over the edge of that runway and finished up in a pile of burning wreckage. It raised questions in my mind about the flying abilities of some of the 'qualified' instructors.

Gaining a little twin-engine time, I flew to Polbrooke and back to Molesworth in a Bristol Blenheim a few times. Although the aircraft was not difficult to fly, I felt happy that I had been assigned to single-engine duties. The Blenheim did not display the handling qualities that I had become used to in single-engine fighter aircraft. I'm becoming snobbish, aren't I?

It was not surprising during flight training that some trainees decided that flying was not for them and dropped out voluntarily, possibly perceiving that the danger was more than they could handle, but why did it take so long before they found out? I had expected at times, and even hoped, I could drop out, but I suppose I was either growing up or losing my mind by becoming hardened to the danger of flying. I felt completely at home in the sky performing aerobatics and revelling in the pure enjoyment of swimming in the air as I, termed the art of flying. I had practised aerobatics to the point that I felt that I did not have a great deal more to learn and, when instructed to take a Miles Master and perform aerobatics manoeuvres for an hour, I felt that the hour could be put to better use by indulging in the more pleasurable exercise of flying to 21 EFTS where I had first soloed. I felt that it would cement in my own mind the progress that I had made and I asked permission to do that instead of performing aerobatics. I was unceremoniously told, 'NO, go and perform aerobatics.' Feeling somewhat chaffed by the curt negative response, I boarded my aeroplane, a Miles Master Mk 3, and although some non-essential instruments were not working I decided that the aircraft was acceptable for flight and signed the flight authorisation book together with the Form 700 accepting the aircraft. After the usual preliminaries, I taxied to the active runway and took off, climbing to an altitude of 5,000 feet and started performing aerobatics as instructed. However, feeling chagrined about the snappy answer to my request and the abrupt instruction to go and do aerobatics, I was rebellious and, instead of performing aerobatics some distance away, I performed a loop directly over the airfield at 5,000 feet. Being unaware of any regulations in KRs or ACIs that prohibited aerobatics over the airfield, provided they were accomplished within the specified heights and ending at not less than 3,000 feet above ground level, I then climbed vertically through a thin layer of stratus cloud, returning in the same manner vertically down through the layer. This was fun and, as the cloud moved away from the airfield, I decided that I would continue performing aerobatics over the field and in my exuberance give any observers on the ground an exhibition of just what an aircraft with a 'competent' (or idiot) pilot could accomplish. For the next hour I performed many different aerobatic manoeuvres, including some that apparently no one had seen before. In addition to square loops, that were done by climbing vertically and rolling out on top and, after flying straight and level inverted for a short distance, descending vertically and rounding out horizontally to the original position. I did these square loops differently, with a twist no one had seen before: on each leg of the loop I performed a 360-degree roll, starting horizontally on the bottom, repeating a 360-degree roll vertically and again a 360-degree roll on the top, another 360 on the vertical down leg and, after rolling out on the horizontal leg, another 360-degree roll, repeating this performance non-stop for a considerable period of time, each time noting to my satisfaction that I was hitting my slipstream which assured that each loop was perfectly symmetrical. After an hour and a quarter of continual aerobatic manoeuvres, I decided that it was enough as the effort was not only tiring me but also the aeroplane and took it down to a perfect landing. As I taxied I applied power to surmount a ridge in the taxiway and the tail lifted off the ground. Fortunately I instantly pulled the control column back to prevent the propeller from striking the ground, it saving me from an embarrassing moment together with the chewing out that I knew I was going to get when I returned to the flight office. I was pretty sure I had not contravened any regulations that could warrant a court martial but the reception I expected from the Chief Flying Instructor would hardly be termed warm. The Chief Flying Instructor did not start by immediately chewing me out. Indeed I was quite surprised when he said that the exhibition that I had displayed was such that a court martial had been considered but, after reviewing the performance, he admitted that the display had merit and commented on what he thought had been high-speed stalls, which I pointed out were fluctuations of flight as I hit my own slipstream and were evidence of the accuracy of my manoeuvres. It transpired that the aerobatic display must have been impressive because when the course graduated shortly afterwards and were awarded the Royal Air Force pilot's flying badge (pilot's wings), I received the only 'above average' assessment, an assessment rarely given. It appeared that sometimes bending the rules could be beneficial; in this case that assumption had proved correct, although perhaps my brinkmanship was rather like skating on thin ice.

When we returned to Ternhill with the advancement in our status of training there did seem to be a more relaxed atmosphere; we trainee pilots were provided with a small recreation room where there was bread, butter and jam and a fire where we could make toast. The topic of conversation was predominately of the anticipated change in our status when we would become entitled to wear the wings of RAF pilots and the promotion that would accompany that occasion. Most would be promoted to the rank of sergeant and a few would become officers and be elevated to the rank of pilot officer. Among those who were to be promoted to commissioned rank was Marcelle Lorand of the Free French Air Force, together with another pilot by the name of Bob Cherry. However, Bob had become embroiled in a fight on an air force bus while in transit from the satellite field at Chetwynd to Ternhill and his promotion to commissioned rank was cancelled. I, of course, had never considered myself to be of commissionable material and was not surprised by not being considered. However, I felt highly complimented when Marcelle Lorand said that he would much rather have been assessed as 'above average' than be promoted to commissioned rank. In a way I was somewhat embarrassed but was happy that being considered 'above average' was held in such high esteem. Considering where I had come from in life, and my motivation for joining the RAF, I was doubly happy that I had been able to finish the course and would be promoted to the rank of sergeant and that the difficulties were being left behind. I felt modestly happy that I was to be awarded pilot's wings and would become officially a Royal Air Force pilot. Recalling when I was enrolled in infants' school and wrote that first composition on what I wanted to do when I grew up, 'To fly an Aeroplane', it was now a dream come true and I had been the only one assessed 'above average' (can you see how modest I am?). From this childhood dream of flying in an old biplane of the 1920s to actually becoming a pilot of modern aircraft was not only a dream come true but, also, the assessment of 'above average' reinforced my feeling of self-confidence. Although aware that I had become competent in my flying skills I had never considered that I could accomplish something better that others; I was contented. Despite the risks, I was still happy that my reason for joining the Royal Air Force had matured in such a satisfactory way. I no longer needed an aeroplane – I was walking on air! I no longer felt like an uncouth kid.

Being used to being told what to do, it came as a surprise when I was asked to indicate the type of flying activities I would like to be assigned to after graduation. I had expected to be ordered to whatever assignment they chose according to what the needs of the time were. Being unexpectedly asked what my preferences were left me at a loss as to what to answer; my thoughts had not roved that far into the future and I had never anticipated being asked what I would like to do.

The only thought that immediately entered my mind was that, although I was about to be become a qualified as an air force pilot, flying a large bomber was a skill far removed from the experience I had of piloting single-engine aircraft, and having gained pleasurable experience flying the Hawker Hurricane, my desire was to be recommended for a posting where I could fly fighter aircraft, especially a Spitfire, but I felt it presumptive to ask for such an assignment. However, I had to request something and in my own mind a Spitfire was an aircraft that only the elite of pilots would be privileged to fly, and I did not consider myself in that class. But I had to say something, so I ventured, 'Could I get a posting where I could fly Spitfires, Sir?' I was not quite sure what the answer was, but it included photographic reconnaissance and, in a jumbled state of mind, I did not realise that this unexpected need to make a decision could have serious consequences. But the question had been sprung upon me so totally unexpectedly. I therefore affirmed a choice of photographic reconnaissance as it seemed the most promising possibility of a posting to a Spitfire squadron. Strange circumstance is perhaps what creates a spy but to be a spy in the sky (I later heard it described as playing Russian roulette with five of the chambers loaded) meant the hazard of flying an unarmed aircraft in enemy skies in broad daylight, but I did not know that at the time. In any case they probably would not take any notice of any individual request, and postings would be made as dictated by the current needs of the air force. I felt that if they were to be guided by the evaluation of the individual's flying skills, which in my case was my ability to manoeuvre a fighter aircraft, that would probably be the deciding factor, and I would in all probability be assigned to a fighter squadron. In any case such decisions seemed to be capricious as I had learned from past experience, but placing myself in danger was hardly something that I had in mind when I had volunteered for the Royal Air Force and in a perverted way that, too, was funny.

Despite the bad weather and all the other factors that had caused delays, the course had eventually concluded at No. 5 SFTS and, at long last, the day had arrived when we would be able assume our new ranks and rates of pay. Although the advanced flying course had now ended, it had proved very costly in personnel due to the loss of so many students and instructors who had lost their lives in accidents; the number of pilots who graduated was but a small percentage of those who were enrolled at the beginning of the course.

The identity cards and records of the new pilots were updated to show their new rank and status as Royal Air Force pilots but they were told not to wear their new rank badges or pilots' wings until after leaving Ternhill: this was the practice at the time. Some of the more affluent non-commissioned airmen had bought sergeant-pilot uniforms, tailored for them in Market Drayton. Although they could not wear them until after leaving Ternhill, the uniforms were lined and were a luxurious replacement for the ill-fitting serge of the regular issue uniforms. Of course, the newly commissioned officers already had their new uniforms, had been discharged as enlisted men, and were now enrolled in RAF records as commissioned officers, entitled to assume their new status and use the officers' mess while still at RAF Ternhill. Such was the privilege of rank.

Except for the newly-commissioned officers, we received verbal instructions to attend a special parade. True to type I did not show up; the ones who did were detailed for extra duty delaying their departure by one day. Those detailed for extra duty could wear their new rank of sergeant, together with their wings. The duty that they were assigned was to act as pallbearers at the funerals of seven airmen who had been killed when their Wellington bomber crashed on the approach to Ternhill. I had flown through the smoke from the crash on the last approach that I had made there. 'Titch' Beasley (he had been nicknamed 'Titch' because if a Hurricane landed and appeared to have no pilot, it was Titch who was not tall enough to be seen over the edge of the cockpit) had made arrangements to go to London with Oswald Chan who, of course, was always referred to as 'Charley' after the moving picture character Charley Chan. Titch and Charley had become close friends; Charley had not been selected for the extra duty but Titch had, which ruined their plans to go to London together. Titch felt it was unfair that he had been selected while I had missed the parade and was off the hook. Anyway, I liked them both and told Titch that it was a good thing that I had missed the parade, or I might not have been able to trade places with him and enable them to go to London as they had planned. Could this really be me – doing niceties for other people? But the next day I found that no good deed shall go unpunished; I was to perform double duty and be a pallbearer for two of the unfortunate crew of the crashed Wellington.

As pallbearers, wearing our new rank of sergeant together with the wings of Royal Air Force pilots, it provided a more dignified funeral for the unfortunate crash victims and their bereaved families. It was sad to have to perform the task of burying those unfortunate airmen in a nearby cemetery, but at last we were free to go on leave and for most of us catch a train home from Market Drayton. On the platform at the railway station were the newly-minted RAF pilots, together with the relatives of the unfortunate Wellington bomber's crew. As new sergeant pilots we could not help being exuberant after having survived and graduated from the gruelling training that we had been subjected to for the last several months. Although showing it in front of the grieving relatives was in poor taste, it did seem to provide a little uplift for them to see these young pilots who would now be taking the place of their lost kin.

There was a sense of relief to have graduated. Apart from the ones who were either suspended or had dropped out from the fifty of us who had started the course, many others had been killed in crashes. In addition to the trainees who were killed, approximately twelve instructors had also died in crashes. The strain on both instructors and aircraft in the need to train pilots in the shortest possible time, together with coping with all the difficult weather conditions that had prevailed, had incurred a high cost. Being proud of having fulfilled my childhood dream and wearing the uniform of a Royal Air Force sergeant pilot, I still had an uncomfortable feeling of guilt because of the unintended circumstance that had caused it. Although trying to avoid conscription into the Army, I think I might have been delighted to have been selected for pilot training, but failing the selection interviews twice? Anyway, I could now go home and, maybe, just maybe, I would be looked upon with a little less suspicion of being a shady character now that I was a sergeant pilot in the RAF. On arrival home my mother, contrary to my expectations, instead of expressing concern for what I was doing was obviously proud of me and appeared to have trust in my capabilities. This provided relief from any guilt that I felt regarding her concern for my safety.

They had not been able to turn me into Superman, but I did feel I had become Superboy!

Chapter 5

A Holiday at Blackpool

The three weeks' leave after graduation was not wasted worrying about what my next assignment would be and I relaxed, using the time to find my way around the country in my Ford Eight car, hopefully without getting lost in the absence of any signposts. I spent the three weeks taking a trip through Coventry, Stratford upon Avon and the Vale of Evesham to the West Country, Devon and the Bay of Torquay. Prior to the war my travels were just a few half-crown evening excursions to Skegness from the Great Northern station on Belgrave Road in Leicester. My life in the RAF had opened my eyes to the countryside, something I would love to explore fully in the future – if I were to have one. After returning to Leicester with little to do, my boredom was abruptly changed when Sid Johnson and Tony Scott showed up, Sid from Cliffe Pypard after completing elementary flying training as part of his glider-pilot training and Tony on leave from the Merchant Navy after being promoted from midshipman to second mate. Needless to say, we metaphorically set our home town on fire and, after a week or so of having a riproaring time spending what little pay we had saved, Sid reported back to 6th Airborne Division and Tony to his Anglo-American oil tanker. But my orders, instead of being assigned to a fighter Operational Training Unit (OTU) as I had anticipated, were to report to No. 3 School of General Reconnaissance at RAF Station Squires Gate, Blackpool.

Wondering how this posting could have anything to do with flying fighters I walked from the Blackpool railway station to Squires Gate in the company of a rather rotund and, to me, elderly squadron leader. It was dark and the squadron leader told me that his name was Sunnox; he appeared to be a jovial type and talked to me more as an equal than as an officer to an NCO; whilst I enjoyed this new status of pilot to pilot, nonetheless I was careful to show the proper respect in my replies. The squadron leader jovially related what a great time he was having and referred to his wife humorously as the 'Dragon'. For some reason unbeknown to me he was treating me more as a friend rather than just another service pilot even though we had never met before. Squadron Leader Sunnox revelled in telling me a story that in the Great War he had been a naval officer and claimed to be the only man who had ever looped a submarine which, of course, was a joke, although the story of the creek in the North West Territories of Canada being named after him because he was the first to plot it on a map proved to be true. But wild as he was, 'Tubby', as Squadron Leader Sunnox liked to be called, decidedly gave me the warm feeling of having to some extent bridged the gap between enlisted men and commissioned officers and made me feel more comfortable in the presence of the latter.

I was assigned to a school of general reconnaissance which came as a complete surprise and left me wondering what it had to do with flying fighters? All I could do was wait to find out. After the usual checking in, I was assigned quarters in the Grand Hotel in St Anne's which had been taken over by the RAF to house non-commissioned aircrew members. It was another new experience for me; as I looked at the hotel gardens and the view of the Irish Sea I thought what a wonderful war I was having. Here I am in what had been a first-class hotel; the rooms, although now sparsely furnished, were comfortable and had the luxury of meals being served in the dining room by members of the Women's Auxiliary Air Force (WAAF). This was a standard of living that I certainly had not experienced in the past. The hotel was a few miles away from the airfield but getting to it was more of a pleasure than a chore; it was just one block to the main road to board a double-decker bus that plied a route past the sand dunes to Squires Gate every few minutes, and was a pleasant ride. Waiting for the bus, I was amused to read a school sign that said 'Finishing school for girls preparatory for boys'. Mmm? This was more of a paid holiday than a duty and for frosting on the cake there were aeroplanes to fly not only for free, but being paid to do it. Although I did not know why I was at Squires Gate I was happy that joining the air force had turned out to be so satisfactory. Approaching the aerodrome I noticed the tail of an aircraft with two vertical stabilisers protruding up behind the fence bearing the insignia of the United States Army Air Forces; it was a B-25 Mitchell bomber. It impressed upon me that this was no longer a private war, it was becoming a global conflict. Little did I realise that I would become more closely acquainted with B-25s later.

The RAF station at Squires Gate had once been a horse racetrack but was now occupied by Coastal Command of the Royal Air Force and I was informed that I was now a member of that command. The purpose of this assignment, I was informed, was to teach me to become a navigator. I had not known previously that pilots of Coastal Command were also trained as navigators. But I flew single-engine fighters and there was no room to do anything but find your way around with a map. Although the posting was a surprise, it suited me perfectly; the threat of possible combat operations was pushed off into the future and gave me time to try and find out what Coastal Command had to do with flying fighters.

Considering all the fringe benefits that were accruing I found Blackpool, a well-known seaside resort, an ideal posting for enjoyment and relaxation. Riding the gondola trams along the seafront to Fleetwood was a welcome contrast to the stress of pilot training at No. 5 SFTS. Navigation instruction was provided with lectures interspersed with training flights to practise what we had learned by flying around the Irish Sea in Blackburn Bothas.

To maintain and expand pilot flying skills the new students were encouraged to take advantage of any opportunity to fly as pilots. I was given instruction by Flight Lieutenant Bill Aston in the complexities (perhaps I should say miseries) of flying the heavy twin-engine Blackburn Botha. The aircraft had been designed to carry an 18-inch torpedo internally and be powered by two Taurus engines of approximately 1,100hp, but since those engines were in demand for operational bombers with a higher priority they were not available for the Botha which was instead powered by two Pegasus engines, each of which was 200hp less than the Taurus engine; this left the large heavy unwieldy torpedo bomber very short on power. Due to the size of the massive undercarriage, retracting or extending it required flying this piece of junk – excuse me, aircraft – around the circuit twice just to accomplish one take off and landing. You are probably getting the feeling that I did not like that machine. You would be right, and nor did anyone else. After Hurricanes, flying this unwieldy machine took all the fun out of flying; it was a relief just to get it back on the ground. Flight Lieutenant Bill Aston was a fun guy to fly with but, while trying to take off in Blackburn Botha designated '4E', I followed the correct procedure and advanced the right throttle ahead of the left to help keep it straight as it gathered speed but, even with full left rudder, I still could not keep it straight on the take-off roll. Bill Aston, in the right-hand seat, closed the throttles and, after coming to a stop, changed seats with me, said 'I'll show you how to do it' and taxied the aircraft back to the take-off position. When Bill advanced the throttles, he received a nasty shock: he found that not only could he not keep it straight, he could not even keep it on the runway, let alone get it off the ground. Before he could bring it to a stop he barely missed another Botha that had been left on the grass alongside the runway with a flat tyre. This may sound as if it was a bit hazardous (it was), but Bill and I both thought the whole incident laughable (although what there was to laugh about I don't know). Oddly enough this cemented a longlasting friendship between Bill and me and our paths crossed many times both during and after the war. In the past Botha 4E had had both engines, propellers and fuel systems changed to try and remove its shortcomings, but the shortcomings persisted, making it so notorious that no one wanted to fly it. When it crashed on the beach amongst the sand dunes we all breathed a sigh of relief that the crew had escaped unhurt but were happy that the miserable aircraft was written off and we no longer would have to fly it.

But there were other Bothas and it was still necessary to fly in them. The navigator's position was in a tiny compartment on the port side under the wing, it had restricted visibility and reeked of 'castor oil'. Although I was not prone to airsickness, I did once succumb to the overpowering smell of the castor oil and, although I completed the navigational exercise correctly, I was reprimanded by the pilot for becoming nauseous. I dismissed the remark thinking 'you can't please all the people all the time', but the pilot probably was not happy to be flying a Blackburn Botha either; he would have been even less happy if he had had to fly in the navigator's compartment instead of the pilot's seat (see plate 7).

I had been dying to get my hands on a single-engine aeroplane again and stopping by at Chetwynd on my way home on leave I was happy to comply with a request to fly a Miles Master that was due for maintenance to Ternhill and return with one that had been serviced. Although it only took fifty minutes to fly to Ternhill and return to Chetwynd with the exchange aircraft it was fun to fly a single-engine aeroplane again after the miserable Blackburn Bothas. When I was asked to perform the task it did my ego good to be recognised as a fully-qualified pilot.

On my return to Squires Gate I enjoyed a night navigation exercise around the Irish Sea in a draughty old but lovable Avro Anson flown by Flight Lieutenant Bill Aston, a pleasant change from the navigation exercises in the Blackburn Bothas. But I still flew the Botha occasionally and once did steep turns around the top of Blackpool Tower. In a navigation exercise in a Botha, I unintentionally exposed the villagers of Aberdaron in North Wales to a little excitement. The assignment required flying the Botha on a course that would take it around Bardsey Island at the tip of the Lleyn peninsula of north Wales at low altitude, very low over the village of Aberdaron, across the Lleyn peninsula, still at a very low altitude, and take photographs of the

Menai Strait before returning to Squires Gate. I would refrain from calling the flight fun but, on a later visit to Aberdaron, I was told that a German bomber had flown right up the beach and over them. It was rumoured that it was flown by a German pilot who had once lived in the area. I suppose I should have told them that it was not a German aircraft with a German pilot, but a British Blackburn Botha. I did not have the heart to disillusion them by spoiling their story of it being a German bomber and let the myth persist; it was more fun that way and I did get a chuckle out of it.

Bill Aston was in command of the Anson flight, and was known as 'Old Uncle Bill Aston and all and all, Old Uncle Bill Aston and all', the ditty taken from 'Scarborough Fair'. Bill Aston's Ansons were all in need of repair, but no one showed any concern about the somewhat substandard condition; there was even a rumour that one had a crack in the main spar but, despite the appropriate entries on the Form 700, they were still considered airworthy and that is all we wanted. It was fun fooling about in the Ansons. Flight Sergeant Carder invited me to go up with him and provide a ride for a few Army officers who had not been in an aeroplane before; as there was only one pilot's seat I sat on the main spar that ran through the fuselage just behind the pilot's seat. Flight Sergeant Carder laughed and said 'Let's give them a thrill, hold on'; he then stalled the aircraft. I got a laugh seeing the look on the Army types faces as they rose into the air an inch or two, restrained by their loose harnesses. The laugh quickly disappeared from my face when the bomb-door handle came undone and smote me sharply on the shin. I should mention that the Anson did not have a hydraulic system and the propellers were fixed-pitch. With no hydraulic system the undercarriage was retracted by winding a handle about 140 turns and extended by turning it 140 turns in the opposite direction. The indicator showing the undercarriage was fully down was two small green balls popping up from tubes in the centre of the instrument panel. The bomb doors were also opened and closed by winding a handle on the right side of the fuselage opposite the pilot's seat, the one that smote me on the shin when the bomb doors accidentally came open; I dutifully wound them closed again despite my painful shin. Now the Army officers were having the last laugh – at my expense. One of the reasons the Avro Anson was so well liked was its docility. Flight Sergeant Carder demonstrated how docile it was by starting both engines and then tying the throttle of one engine in the idle position. He then carefully opened the throttle of the remaining engine to full power, took off and flew round the circuit and landed again, with just one engine.

The only reason to wire the other throttle was to prove the point; naturally the wire was very thin and would not have prevented the throttle being opened if necessary.

In addition to flying other aircraft, I piloted a Westland Lysander (see plate 8), which was easy enough to fly, but found it rather unnerving when the flaps automatically extended; they came down with a noise sounding like a hundred angry housewives rattling saucepans. But there was one piece of information that I was not given: the horizontal stabiliser was also the elevator and, after trimming the aircraft for landing, it was advisable not to open the throttle without turning the trim tab forward or the nose would come up and a stall might be unavoidable. I was glad that I did not attempt a go around.

There was also an activity that satisfied my entrepreneurial spirit, smuggling eggs from the Isle of Man, where they were plentiful, to Squires Gate where they were scarce. The eggs were referred to as 'brussels sprouts' to escape the eye of the customs' inspector stationed at Squires Gate. It either worked or perhaps the customs officer turned a blind eye, which was more likely, but the eggs were for a good cause; they were distributed to the airmen's mess, the NCOs' mess and the officers' mess. Although a little underhanded, because the general population were unable to obtain eggs, it would have been nice to have satisfied their needs as well, but we just did not have a large enough aircraft for that and you can't do everything for everyone – there was a war going on!

The navigation course was thorough and included a requirement for the student to demonstrate his knowledge of astro-navigation; in addition to the theory, the students were required to demonstrate that they were able to obtain a fix (pinpoint where they were) by using lines of position from calculations derived from sights made with a bubble sextant. The trainees were required to demonstrate their capability of using the bubble sextant (used for measuring the declination of heavenly bodies without reference to a horizon); by keeping the bubble in the centre, it enabled readings to be taken at any altitude and, by using a chronometer ('watch' if you had one), establish the exact time that the observation was made. (Have I lost you yet?) The students were required to take ten such sights at ground level and work out the declination of ten different heavenly bodies (stars), after determining their ephemeredes (their locations in the sky), calculate the local hour angle from the first point of Aries and plot the lines of position using the observations and the *Naval Astronomical Tables*. By plotting the lines of position and documenting the calculations this showed accomplishment of this requirement. All this could take a considerable period of time which, I considered, like the time you just spent reading about it, was time wasted. If it appears complicated that's because it was, but it was hardly the sort of thing that I would want to stay up late at night hopefully waiting for a clear sky to be able to take the shots. Being of a lazy disposition, it seemed to me to be an awful lot of work, so I figured that, instead of going to all that trouble, I would provide evidence of having accomplished the task without taking the observations, together with the required calculations and satisfy the course requirements. I simply spent a few minutes doing the exercises backwards without even making the sextant sights and this was a lot simpler than going through all the complicated procedures outlined in the course requirements. This removed the unpleasant task of standing outside in the middle of the night trying to take the ten sights which could take hours, especially waiting for cloudless skies. It seemed obvious to me that there is no point of working if you can find a way of avoiding it. I do not know if anyone checked my 'work' but if they did they would have been just as lost as I was. I am sure glad that I never had to obtain a fix that way – it might have been very tricky in a single-engine fighter.

The paid holiday in Blackpool was enjoyable and the visit by my sister and brother-in-law who themselves spent a week's holiday there was frosting on the cake. What with riding the open gondola trams to Fleetwood and seeing the play *No Orchids for Miss Blandish* with Robert Newton playing the role of Slim Grissom and ice-skating at the skating rink next to the Blackpool ballroom, it lulled me into a feeling that life could not get any better. But it could. I was taught how to skate by a very pretty young lady who said her name was Sonia Bowes-Lyon. I was later informed that Bowes-Lyon was the maiden name of the Queen. I wondered if Sonia really could have been a member of the royal family? I was told that members of the Bowes-Lyon family had moved to Blackpool from the Channel Islands, which had been occupied by the Germans, but things like that may happen in the pictures but not in real life to people like me – could they? Being taught to ice skate by a princess, although I did not know that at the time! When I found out who she was, my head was filled with disbelief and I dismissed it as a coincidence of names. I had things backwards anyway. She had actually taught me to skate backward before I learned to skate forward but, thanks to Sonia, I did become proficient as an ice skater. But, speaking of Royalty, I recalled while in the Link Trainer at Ternhill that the instructor had told me to stay in the trainer. When I was told I could come out, I asked why I had been told to stay in and he told me that the 'Monarch' (King George VI) had come in to see the operation. I was happy that the circuit trace on the instructor's table showed the line of the take off was connected with the line of the landing; well some days you just get lucky and I did feel rather privileged to be in the presence of the King, even if I did not see him. Then again, I thought perhaps the instructor might have been playing a joke on me, but the King was visiting the station that day and it almost enabled me to be a name dropper.

But as a back-street kid turned pilot, I all too soon had become qualified as a navigator but, even though the report stamped in my logbook stated 'Greater concentration and keenness would have bettered my results', I wondered how I could have bettered the results when the results were (in my opinion) 'perfect'. My 'holiday' at Squires Gate was coming to a close when it was confirmed that I was destined to have a career (hopefully not a short one) flying Spitfires – as a photographic reconnaissance pilot. I had run out of ideas of how to turn the unexpected qualifications of being both a Royal Air Force pilot and a navigator into something less dangerous than flying into the jaws of death. But my fear was now tempered with the feeling that someone has to turn the tide of war in the favour of the Allies, but does it have to be me? (I really did not think I could do it alone.) The idea of joining the RAF to avoid conscription into the Army had certainly worked; it had worked with a vengeance. Being apprehensive about facing the enemy was something that I supposed all aircrew had; I hoped that in me it was not a sign of cowardice. Were cowards aware of being cowards or was it something that was sorted out when the wheat was separated from the chaff? Although it was against my code of ethics to shoot someone without even the benefit of a formal introduction, it was not a cloak to cover a streak of cowardice (said he, hopefully). Fear of unknown danger was normal, but even bombing attacks lost some of the terror as people became accustomed to them. When the time came I knew that I would face the enemy and hoped that I might be seen as a better character than the one which I appeared to have been in the past. The saying has it that a coward dies a thousand deaths; oh well, on the bright side I still have a few hundred left to go! I still had concern for my mother who must be worried about my brother (William) who was in India; it was sad that she had to face the possible loss of one or both of her sons in the future. It was bad enough that her husband had been killed on the Somme during the Great War without her having concern due to the activities in which her sons were now engaged. But she was British, and a stalwart woman who showed pride rather than fear; she knew fighting a war is a dirty job that had to be done, a danger shared by the peoples of so many countries. Growing up in wartime was probably very different to what it would have been in peacetime; it was the way things were and, if nothing else, I am not in Dartmoor – yet! My current circumstances conflicted with my former attitude of looking out for myself, although it now seemed to be more important to look out for everyone else and all I had tried to do was avoid conscription into the Army and sit out the war in safety – but that was before. At the moment there were no decisions to make, danger loomed ahead, and I was on a one-way street. The time to pay the piper was getting closer. Despite having developed into someone who would not avoid the danger of operational flying, please forgive my being unable to claim that I was thrilled with the idea. But I would bravely face the enemy when that time came (said he with his fingers crossed). There might be people who were now looking up to me and although this may have been a mistaken summation of my character on their part, it would leave me with a feeling of betrayal if I failed to measure up to what was now expected of me. But why should I concern myself about them? I doubt if they would want to trade places with me or exhibit the standards that they expected of me. But laugh if you will, I would not trade places with them either. Did all members of the military or for that matter anyone facing danger have these same conflicting thoughts and self doubts? It was useless to ask others how they felt as I knew if I asked they would deny having fears the same as I would, and perhaps laugh about it. With all these thoughts I decided to let the dice fall where they might and I would just have to make the best of it (as if I had any choice). Enough of these doubts, bring on the enemy, said he laughingly, be merry for tomorrow we – oh I don't want to continue with that!

Chapter 6

Gateway to Hell

War did strange things, such as changing clueless kids into
pilots and commanders of warplanes in just a few months,
but that was the way it was.

The last step in being trained for operations as a photographic reconnaissance pilot was conducted at an operational training unit (OTU) and hopefully with the reward of flying a Spitfire. However, this was tempered by the impending danger of operations against the enemy that would follow, but danger provides character, said I with a shrug. The experience to be gained at the Operational Training Unit would contribute to providing confidence in performing the tasks that lay ahead, even if photographic reconnaissance was considered by some to contain an 'element' of danger. But phooey to danger, who's scared – don't look at me like that. I'm just cold!

The posting to No. 8 (PR) OTU did not come as a surprise, although I did wonder if I had been assigned to photographic reconnaissance because I had indicated a preference for that rather than being assigned to duties as a fighter pilot. Or could it be there were no other volunteers for PRU? The training unit was located close to Fraserburgh in Scotland. Although it was the last step before being posted to an operational squadron, the posting itself posed no threat and did mean I might get to fly a Spitfire, which would be an unprecedented reward if that happened (wow, me flying a Spitfire?). The airfield was situated on the edge of nowhere and, although fairly primitive, it did have runways, one sloping down toward the North Sea and ending only a few feet from the water (a proximity for which later I would be grateful), separated by only by a few rocks and a narrow-gauge railway line. The Fraserburgh-Cairnbulg-Inverallochy and St Coombs Light Railway was a rather quaint narrow-gauge railway that was used by the locals and airmen to travel between Cairnbulg-Inverallochy and Fraserburgh. Accommodation at the airfield was in typical huts that had become common at military installations and which were spread around a crossroads. The sergeants' mess was on the east side of the road leading to Fraserburgh with the flight headquarters located in a hut on the airfield. Security was light and, the aerodrome being located in such a remote and inconspicuous place, it lent a more relaxed feeling to the base.

I had brought my Montgomery motorcycle to Fraserburgh on the train, and found it useful to ride into the 'Brock', as Fraserburgh was known colloquially. It was also useful to tow other pilots on their bicycles, hanging on to a rope tied around the saddle post in vic formation. The aircraft dispersal, located on the far side of the airfield, was a long way to ride a bicycle; yes aeroplanes were provided but no transportation to get to them. In command of the OTU was an officer by the name of Lord Malcolm Douglas-Hamilton, a wing commander who had a penchant for taking long walks to the top of the nearest mountain or high point. Although there can be little objection to such activity, I was not overjoyed by the mandatory inclusion of all the station flying personnel. I did try but I was unable to avoid it. However, it probably was an enhancement to the health of the participants – if they did not die of exhaustion. The flight schedule was to prepare the pilots for their conversion to Spitfires; the Spitfire, as with the Hurricane, was a single-seat fighter and thus could only be flown solo and without a check ride. The flight characteristics of the Spitfire were simulated as nearly as possible using Miles Master Mk 3 aircraft. The characteristics were simulated by making landing approaches with the instructor in the front cockpit and the student flying the aircraft from the rear cockpit with his seat lowered to minimise the forward view. This simulated the lack of forward visibility over the nose of the Spitfire, necessitating a curved approach so that the pilot would be able to see the runway all the way to touchdown. On a straight-in approach the nose of the aircraft prevented him seeing the runway at all. Minimum flap extension was used with the Master as the flaps on a Spitfire, with its elliptical wing, provided only drag, not lift. After several such flights I was able to simulate Spitfire approaches in the Miles Master and demonstrate that I was capable of flying a Spitfire and able to cope with the Spitfire's narrow undercarriage, a problem for some pilots when landing.

I was confident that I could handle the aeroplane and stuck my neck out by asking if I could be the first on the course to fly a Spitfire (secretly I had always wanted to be first at something). The answer was 'yes'. I accomplished the pre-flight walk-round inspection and climbed into the cockpit of Spitfire Mk III X4599, adjusted my position in the cockpit and moved the rudder pedals by turning the large nut between the pedals with my heel to suit my leg length. After closing the cockpit entry flap, I signalled that I was ready to start the Rolls Royce Merlin engine; the APU (auxiliary power unit) plugged into the power receptacle on the side of the aircraft provided power to turn the engine over and was the normal method of starting the engine (if an APU was not available the onboard battery was capable of starting it). After turning the ignition switches on and pressing the booster and starter buttons, the engine turned over and caught, settling into the deep-throated roar characteristic of the Merlin. The mechanic removed the APU connection and I was on my own to make my first flight in a Spitfire. Having checked the instruments, I was satisfied that oil pressure, oil and coolant temperatures, the pneumatic pressure (pneumatic pressure was essential for the operation of the brakes and flaps) were correct. Because I was intending to fly at an altitude of more than 15,000 feet, I also turned on the oxygen supply to 100 per cent. With the checks completed, I waved the chocks away, taxied to the active runway and checked the trim-tab indicator, the magnetoes and that the propeller was in full fine pitch. After adjusting the seat to the full-up position to provide maximum forward visibility over the long nose, I lined up with the runway ready to advance the throttle for take off. There was no tower or for that matter radios. With no need for a take-off clearance, as I opened the throttle the aircraft seemed to have a mind of its own. I was able to see straight down the runway as the tail raised off the ground in the slipstream and it waggled as though saying 'Oh goodie, we're going to fly'. As the speed increased on the take-off roll the controls came to life and I knew this was an aircraft I was going to love. After leaving the ground I lowered the seat and retracted the undercarriage, closed the canopy and, after adjusting the boost rpm and trimming the aircraft, I climbed out of the circuit feeling completely at ease. During the climb I thought back to before the war started and I had read in a paper about a boy who had stood at the edge of an aerodrome marvelling at the sight of a Spitfire taking off and thinking how wonderful it would be to fly one. The intervention of war created just that opportunity; soon afterwards he became a Spitfire pilot. With the wonderful deep-throated roar of the Merlin engine in my ears, I recalled the day I had cycled to Desford and stood at the edge of the aerodrome against the 'Trespassers will be prosecuted' sign looking wistfully at the aeroplanes, thinking how wonderful it must be to fly, and now, somehow, fate had intervened in the same way as the boy in the *Eagle* comic. It had happened to me, I was flying a Spitfire, my world was complete. But the 'Trespassers will be prosecuted' sign at Desford stuck in my mind, together with the admonition that was misquoted by a friend as 'Trespassers will be propped up and shot'. I wondered if perhaps I had crossed that imaginary line and was now trespassing into forbidden territory, not a comforting thought. Although having failed the aircrew selection interview twice and having been found of unsuitable material for training as an aircrew member, I wondered how fate had brought me to this point and flying a Spitfire, a fate about which I certainly did not have any complaint. I listened to the steady drone of the engine and practised manoeuvres to familiarise myself with the handling qualities of the aircraft before climbing into the heavens of 30,000 feet. At the indicated climb speed of 162 mph a rate of climb was provided of almost 3,000 feet per minute at low altitudes, but the rate of climb reduced to less than 1,000 feet a minute as higher altitudes were reached; this made the climb to 30,000 feet take about half an hour. On reaching that altitude, although the controls were now somewhat sluggish, the breathtaking view provided in the thin air was something I hadn't anticipated and it seemed as though I could see forever. The maximum height that I had flown previously had been 15,000 feet and now I was at an altitude twice that high, higher even than the top of Mount Everest, higher than any place on earth, literally miles higher than I had ever been before. But there was a drawback to flying at high altitude in an unpressurised aircraft; even with 100 per cent oxygen the pilot was unable to absorb enough oxygen which resulted in some degradation of his mental reactions. Above 35,000 feet consciousness would be lost in just a short period of time despite maximum oxygen flow. These considerations did not concern me during the hour or more I spent revelling in my newfound love and reluctantly returned to Fraserburgh. After lowering the undercarriage and flaps, I made the curved approach to the runway, held off close to the ground and slowly closed the throttle, allowing the aircraft to gently kiss the ground in a perfect three-point landing, I knew then that the Spitfire and I would become great friends. The following weeks were filled familiarising myself with characteristics of the Spitfire and flying cross-country exercises where I was free to roam far and wide over an extensive area of the northern part of the British Isles to my heart's content.

The town of Fraserburgh was a typical Scottish fishing town situated at the north-east corner of Aberdeenshire where local boat builders had turned their skills from building fishing boats to wooden minesweepers. Alongside the docks a number of brick and concrete air-raid shelters had been built which came in useful for a purpose for which they were not intended. While riding my motorcycle with a dog relentlessly trying to nip my left ankle

I brushed close to one of the air-raid shelters. The dog, concentrating on biting my ankle, failed to see the air-raid shelter looming in its path. Knowing it was irresistible for a dog not to chase a motorcyclist's ankles, I hoped the dog did not have too much of a headache after its sudden stop. Despite the remoteness of the town the contribution that the local population put into the war effort was impressive: it seemed that they did everything from providing seafood from fishing to building big minesweepers, but there was little to do in the evening. Going to see a film at the local cinema would fill the occasional evening but there was little else to do; Fraserburgh would not be considered a hive of entertainment. Having watched a film that stared Elsa Lanchester and Charles Laughton, I enjoyed the picture but, after leaving the cinema, I found the town closed for the night; there was not even a place to get a cup of tea or fish and chips. Despite the lack of things to do Fraserburgh left me with warmth that could only have been derived from the solid community and the spirit displayed by this wonderful Scottish town.

Have you ever danced a Scottish reel? I did in one of the villages of Cairnbulg and Inverallochy. I was sober but it still made my head spin trying to dance a 'Dashing White Sergeant' or an 'Eightsome Reel'. I do not know which of the villages the hall was in because the two villages appeared to be one; traffic was non-existent as there were no streets, just a pathway connecting them to the main road. It would have been a longer walk to catch a bus, so the residents would ride to town on the light railway that connected the towns of Fraserburgh, Cairnbulg/Inverallochy and St Coombs. If passengers were waiting the train driver would stop for them; there was no station or platform and it required a rather large step up to enter the carriages. Returning from Fraserburgh to the airfield on the train one afternoon the engine driver invited me to ride on the footplate. Following the driver's instructions I drove the train back to Cairnbulg/Inverallochy thinking 'Spitfire pilot to railway engine driver all in one day, life can't be all bad!' Being stationed in an out of the way corner of Scotland had its compensations and certainly provided a broadened perspective on life.

The weekend motorcycle rides to the fascinating Scottish city of Aberdeen were also fun, although I felt relieved when I reached the Bridge of Dee on the northern edge of Aberdeen without freezing to death. Riding a motorcycle for over an hour in the cold Scottish climate would even make an iceberg feel cold. A chance meeting with Sergeant Grey created a pleasant weekend. Sergeant Grey and I had met before and he was kind enough to invite me to stay at his mother's home in Aberdeen. It was comforting to spend a few hours in the warmth of a home after the austerity of life at an air force base. Sergeant Grey told me that he was flying some type of intruder operations using twin-engine Douglas Bostons. After I told him that I had volunteered for photographic intelligence sorties he appeared concerned and tried to convince me that I should volunteer for some other type of assignment, pointing out that when in the company of other aircraft you were only a small percentage of a target but as a lone photographic aircraft you are 100 per cent of the target, and an unarmed one at that. Although it had been an enjoyable weekend and I had enjoyed Sergeant Grey's hospitality, I was glad that he was happy flying the type of operations he was comfortable with, but I would rather not have heard his comparison of dangers associated with flying photographic reconnaissance compared to what he was doing.

Warrant Officer Robert Black, an American citizen enrolled as a pilot in the Royal Air Force, had been flying Hampden bombers before his posting to Fraserburgh where he was awaiting his transfer to the United States Army Air Forces. Bob and I would venture out from the small beach at the end of the runway onto the cold waters of the North Sea in a 'Foldboat' (a folding canoe that Mr Harrison had lent me); out in the open sea we would try to catch fish that apparently knew more about evasive action than we did. Although a warrant officer, off duty the talk was informal, both of us using each other's first names. We were fairly far from shore seeking the elusive fish when a number of dots appeared on the eastern horizon. As they came closer, they turned directly toward us; the silhouette of the aircraft resembled German Dornier 217s. Fortunately, as Bob and I were about to extend our search for the fish into their own environment, Bob recognised that of all things it was a squadron of Handley Page Hampden bombers, the type of aircraft that he had been flying until recently. Having barely escaped getting wet we chose not to make any further search for those elusive fish who were probably laughing at us anyway.

The routine of training continued and I must have led a charmed life by staying out of trouble as I flew Spitfire X4326, a Mk 1a, on a cross country exercise; the weather was good with excellent visibility and I decided to fly at low altitude and explore the countryside. I flew inland before turning south over wooded rugged countryside and wondered what the baronial mansion with a square tower was as I passed over at low altitude, pondering what the flag flying high on the tower flagpole was for. After reaching the Firth of Forth I looked down on the Forth Bridge; it looked so impressive in the afternoon sunlight and I revelled in how wonderful it was to be able to fly. After circling over the firth and passing over the Rosyth Royal Naval Dockyard, I headed back on the return leg to Fraserburgh. As I flew north the daylight was beginning to fade and on arrival over the aerodrome at Fraserburgh it was early dusk but, even without instrument panel lights, the feel of the controls was enough to land, but it was still light enough to read the instruments anyway. However, as I came close to touchdown I saw vehicles moving and feared that they might get into my landing path and climbed back to circuit altitude. I watched the vehicles being moved into a line alongside the runway and saw that they had lights on. At this point I realised that they were in effect providing an electric flare path which annoyed me because, had they not interfered, I would have been on the ground and on my way to the mess for supper. The touchdown was perfect as usual, but it was irritating to have to be careful not to hit those dammed vehicles with the lights they had put at the side of the runway and, although there was no lecture, I presumed they realised that I had more confidence in my ability than they apparently had. However, I was curious about the mansion that I had flown over and asked if anyone knew what it was. I was told it could only have been Balmoral Castle and that the flag on the tower indicated that the King and family were in residence. Flying over Balmoral Castle with King George VI in residence was a definite no-no and a court martial offence. But there was no need to worry; I had flown over it so fast and so low that it would not have been possible for anyone to identify the aircraft number. I was chuffed to be able to enter a night landing in my logbook, something not every Spitfire pilot was able to do. Spitfires were not equipped for night flying and few Spitfire pilots would need to make night landings unless they goofed up, as I had. Flying activities were interspersed with high-level cross-countries, low-level oblique photography and photography exercises at high altitude. The flying was interesting but sadly a tragic accident occurred: Sergeant Eastman was killed when he crashed into a mountainside obscured by fog. The lowering cloud in the valley he was trying to fly through had reduced visibility to zero.

We were now practising high-level photography over Scotland and Northern Ireland in the same way that we would carry out aerial espionage over enemy territory, but without having the stress of possible interception. One Monday, having just returned from Aberdeen after spending the weekend there, I was assigned a cross-country flight with a turning point over the Mull of Galloway; approaching the Mull at 30,000 feet I noticed the pneumatic pressure was low and pneumatic pressure was essential to operate both the flaps and the brakes. In the event of low pneumatic pressure occurring our orders were to land at the nearest airfield as soon as possible to retain enough pneumatic pressure for a safe landing. The instructions were clear enough but I was at 30,000 feet over the Mull of Galloway, so what comprised the nearest airfield? I made the decision to land at Squires Gate, which was almost within gliding distance, the runways there were familiar to me but the deciding factor was that it had one very long runway, so what better choice was there? On arrival at Squires Gate, I lined up to land on the active runway although it did not appear to be long enough should I encounter any problems. After lowering the undercarriage I selected the 'down' position for the flaps but, to my dismay, only one flap came, down causing the aeroplane to roll to the left. I immediately returned the flap selector to the 'up' position and righted the aircraft. Undaunted, I decided to land without the flaps but found after touch-down that the brakes would not stop me by the end of the runway and opened the throttle to do a go-around and try again. After two more attempts I realised that it would be impossible to stop the aircraft on that short runway before overshooting and running into obstacles at the end of it. The only logical choice I could make was to use the long runway for landing. But it was important to let the ground personnel know of my intent to use the long runway. However, this aircraft, like all the others at the OTU, had no radio, so there was no way to tell anyone that I had to use the long runway.

Newly-built Wellington bombers from the nearby factory were parked on both sides of the runway at the far end, but it was still the only runway that it would be possible to land on without damage. The only way to indicate my need and show my intent of using that runway was by approaching from the sea and flying low along the runway a number of times, waggling my wings; after I felt sure that they had got the message I hoped that ground personnel would clear it of any obstructions before my landing attempt. But it was obvious that there was insufficient time to move the Wellingtons before I could attempt the landing. Satisfied that I had done all I could to prepare for landing, I made my approach, but without flaps my speed was unavoidably fast and, after touchdown, the only way to keep the aircraft straight without brakes was to apply power to create a slipstream over the rudder and provide directional control. But this would extend my landing roll considerably and the only way for the aircraft to be brought to a stop was to wait until it lost momentum and came to a stop on its own. The worrying part was that there would be no room for error as the landing run would end between the parked Wellingtons and keeping the aircraft straight at that point was critical. After careful consideration, I made the first of three attempts and subsequent go-arounds. I discontinued these landing attempts due to being unable to keep the aircraft straight before running out of runway, each resulting in having to go around and try again but, learning from each attempt, I knew that I could get it right in the end and was determined to land the aircraft without damage. The only other way to stop the aeroplane once on the ground would be by retracting the undercarriage. I was not just trying to prevent damage to my aircraft, I was trying to avoid damage to myself. By retracting the undercarriage I could slide into a parked Wellington which would have been a disaster, resulting in my being killed or suffering serious injury and that was not an option I was inclined to take. On the fourth approach to the runway, having learned from each of the three previous attempts, I touched down on the very threshold at just above stalling speed and, with very delicate applications of power, I was able to keep the aircraft straight as it gradually slowed down and, after what seemed to be an eternity, it rolled to a standstill in the centre of the runway between the parked Wellingtons with room left before the end of the runway. I had dealt with the problem thoughtfully with a calm analysis of the situation and it had resulted in a satisfactory outcome. However, I did breathe a sigh of relief and felt good knowing that it had not been just luck and felt happy that I had acquired enough skill to be able to make a successful landing despite the odds.

Selecting Squires Gate was to me the only correct decision as to where I should attempt the landing (see plate 9). It would have been impossible at any other airfield unless it had such a long runway and it was the only airfield I knew of that had one long enough, so what choice did I have? Despite this decision being obvious to me, it was not necessarily the choice that others might have made for me and I had concern that there could be a post-mortem that found that they did not consider that I had made the right decision. But you can't please everyone all the time and I had landed without damage to either the aircraft or myself.

Sitting there with the aircraft stationary a little comic relief was provided by a ground control vehicle pulling in front with a sign on the back that stated 'FOLLOW ME'. The driver had to be joking; taxiing would be like driving a car that had no steering or brakes. However, by using small applications of power, just enough to move the aircraft a few feet at a time, I managed to move the aircraft off the runway to a hardstanding without overheating the engine coolant. That in itself was difficult since a Spitfire could not be taxied far before the coolant temperature would reach 90 degrees centigrade, making it necessary to shut the engine down to avoid damage. The only problem with the aircraft was it not having any pneumatic pressure but it had to be repaired, making it necessary to find a place to spend the night. Having only a little money left after spending the weekend in Aberdeen, and being tired from the effort of making the difficult landing, I just sat around and talked with other pilots. I could have left the station if I wanted as I was wearing a street uniform and not an aircrew uniform (at that time it was not permissible to wear one off base), but wearing a street uniform rather than a flight uniform would come back to haunt me when I returned to Fraserburgh. The following morning there were low clouds and there was no flying activity, but my aircraft had been repaired and I was anxious to return to Fraserburgh as soon as possible. The meteorological office informed me that there was thick cloud up to an altitude of 10,000 feet with clouds to the west, ending in a line running north and south over Scotland with clear skies in the east. With this information I convinced flying control that, although I did not have a radio (as required for the instrument flight), I was perfectly capable of taking off and climbing through the clouds and landing back at Fraserburgh without any problem. The take off and flight were uneventful and the pneumatic pressure remained up, indicating that the pneumatic pressure problem had been fixed, and I continued north to Scotland without concern about having brakes and flaps for landing. During the flight I reviewed my actions of the previous day and was sure that I had used sound judgement by deciding to use my height to reach a familiar airfield with the long runway needed to make a successful landing without damage. I felt lucky to have been able to get out of what I now realised was a very dangerous situation and had avoided any damage, damage for which those who would make up the 'facts' to suit themselves would have condemned me. Landing back at Fraserburgh, I was told to report to the commanding officer where an aura of my being guilty until proved innocent prevailed. The commanding officer put two and two together and came up with five: first I was wearing a regular street uniform instead of a flying uniform, indicating that I had probably intended to land at Blackpool; and, secondly I did not have the means of proving that there had been a pneumatic malfunction. It certainly made it appear possible that I might have flown to Blackpool for the fun of it – but I didn't. But condemnation was better than what the alternative might have been had I not been able to pull off a successful landing. It may have looked suspicious but I could not see any choice other than the one I made. There being a modicum of doubt that I might just have been telling the truth and, although I did not elaborate on the difficulty that I had experienced in landing at Squires Gate, the flying skills I had displayed in overcoming the weather in my effort to return as quickly as possible perhaps dispelled some of the commanding officer's doubts or wrath. The matter was passed off with just the usual tongue lashing, although I rather suspect that he later made himself aware of what had happened at Squires Gate. Well, at least there were no charges made and, in any case, you can't win them all. But guilty or not, you will still only be known by what others think or say about you and at that point, with the self confidence that I was now feeling, I no longer cared, but the commanding officer (Wing Commander Lord Malcolm Douglas-Hamilton) always appeared fair in his decisions. But if the facts were determined, a pat on the back would have been nice. But put yourself in my place; I think you would also feel good after being able to pull that one off.

Accidents, although rarer than at SFTS, still happened. When flying the same route that had been taken by Sergeant Eastman when he had been killed, I ran into identical weather conditions as I flew on a southerly course approaching Newtownmore in the highlands of Scotland. I was concerned by the clouds lowering and forming a small triangular shape between the base of the cloud and the surrounding mountains. In the poor visibility I could see that the valley was rapidly being closed in and decided that the surrounding mountains were too much of a threat to continue flying using visual flight rules. Feeling that discretion was the better part of valour, I went on to instruments and climbed to an altitude higher than the tops of the mountains. Breaking out above the cloud tops I felt thankful that I had evaded the same trap that had lured Sergeant Eastman to his fate in the same spot the week before.

Though I found that unforeseen dangers were inherent in flying, they were to a great extent unavoidable. I had that point emphasised during a low-level cross-country flight over Cape Wrath on the north-west tip of Scotland. Turning to a course for the Orkney Isles where, in turn, I would set a course back to Fraserburgh, encountering cloud obscuring Cape Wrath, I climbed into the cloud flying on instruments to clear the tops of mountains before setting course for the Orkneys. While still on instruments I let down below the base of the clouds over the sea and found the cloud base had now lowered to a height of a few hundred feet. Breaking out of the cloud my senses were jolted when I saw that close by on my starboard side was a Royal Navy County-class cruiser, together with its escort of destroyers. I felt like a target as I observed their guns being trained on me and hoped that perhaps Royal Navy personnel might be better trained in aircraft recognition than some members of another service. But I felt that discretion in this case was again the better part of valour and avoided the possibility of a shoot-first-and-ask-questions-afterwards situation by immediately climbing back into the clouds and changing course. After what I considered a decent period of time to separate myself safely from the possibility of 'friendly' fire, I again descended and broke cloud at an even lower altitude. After identifying my turning point over the Orkney Isles, with the cloud steadily lowering I deemed it prudent to high-tail it back across the Moray Firth to Fraserburgh while there was still some visibility. The cloud base as I crossed the Moray Firth lowered to the point that I was flying so low I was afraid I might hit the water. Unable to visually judge my height above the sea I was relieved to see land looming up just ahead in the gloom. I recognised Kinnaird Head in Aberdeenshire, but I could see the clouds beyond Kinnaird Head were down to the sea; in other words I would have to find my way to the airfield in thick fog. I was happy that my navigation (call it guesswork) on the course to steer across the Moray Firth had led to a landfall so close to the airfield, but I now had to find the airfield and land in this fog, and with no communications I was on my own with no one else to help. I deployed the flaps and reduced my forward speed to 100 mph, a speed that was slow but still fast enough to be able to make sudden manoeuvres. At zero altitude I managed to fly the short distance south along the rocky coastline and recognised a wrecked trawler on a rock. It was located a few hundred feet north of the runway threshold and, now knowing exactly where the runway was, I lowered the undercarriage and turned in to where the threshold should be. In seconds I saw the light railway and, just across it, the threshold of the runway, the rest of it lost in the thick fog. Although the last several minutes had been highly demanding, I did not have time to be scared. My only thoughts as I touched down on the fog obscured runway were to be thankful that the runway threshold was only a few yards from the water and that there were no obstructions between it and the sea. You do have a feeling of relief and are thankful for a lot of luck after surviving something like that.

Taxiing to the flight dispersal in the thick fog was not as difficult as it might seem as all I had to do was follow the edge of the runway to a safe spot where I could then shut down the engine. I did not receive any accolades, probably because, perhaps, I should have recognised the deteriorating weather conditions earlier and returned before visibility had deteriorated into the fog that had made the landing so precarious. Despite the tenacity that I had displayed in completing the assignment it appeared to go unnoticed but that tenacity would serve me well during the next few years.

Before leaving No. 8 Operational Training Unit there was another incident that shocked me. I had entered into a position where I thought I would 'wrap up' the aeroplane at the far end of the runway. It was a very cold day as I made the approach to land on a wet downhill runway. The runway being wet was not unusual and was of no cause for concern but, after a normal touchdown, I was shocked that the brakes failed to slow the aeroplane, by which time it was too late to open the throttle and go around. All I could do was hope that by the time the end of the runway was reached I would have slowed down sufficiently to retract the undercarriage and minimise the damage. I passed the end of the runway at a considerably reduced speed and prepared to retract the undercarriage. But, as I ran onto the grass separating the runway from the airfield boundary, the brakes worked and the aircraft stopped with no damage. I had mistakenly assumed that the brakes had failed, but realised afterwards that the runway was not just wet, it was wet ice, and I was relieved that the ice on the runway had resulted in nothing more than self-recrimination for not having recognised it for what it was.

Still living in fear of officers!

During the time at OTU a fellow sergeant pilot named Jack Dearden and I became friends and discussed at great length many of the myriad concerns and possibilities that the future might hold for us. During these conversations we discussed the fact that all the non-commissioned officers performed flying duties identical to those of pilots who were of commissioned rank and assumed that officers were chosen from the ranks of the well-educated elite. Since our induction into the Royal Air Force we had been trained for aircrew duties in the company of men from all walks of life, including, amongst others, a Glasgow Corporation bus driver, together with people like myself whose only education was that needed to deliver bread. There were very few among us with a higher education, if any. It appeared to me that this mix was probably a representation of what wartime operational aircrews would consist of and this prompted the thought that the ratio of commissioned officers to non-commissioned enlisted personnel would widen due to the swelling number of conscripted and volunteer personnel. We concluded that relatively few personnel directly entered the RAF as commissioned officers compared to the number of enlisted men and would eventually create a shortage of officers in proportion to the number of other ranks. If this were so I wondered if there was perhaps a method for enlisted personnel to apply for commissions and help fill this gap: if so – how? By this time I had modified my Leicester accent and assumed the 'toffee-nosed' manner of speech that I imagined the upper class used, although there was no doubt in my mind that a commission would never be granted to such a questionable character as I was, and although we were still fearful of officers, even if it was with tongue in cheek, we thought it might be fun to find out if there was a method. After unobtrusively seeking information, I found that, by submitting a completed (RAF) Form 1020a, enlisted personnel could apply for a commission. Jack and I each submitted a completed Form 1020a, thinking it could do little harm even though it was with tongue in cheek with the thought that only applications from personnel with higher educational standards would be considered. Although Jack and I submitted the completed forms just to see what might happen we did not anticipate that there would be any reaction and the completed forms would duly be despatched to the round file never to be heard of again. Our conversations were mostly about the different models of Spitfires that we had become familiar that included the Mk I, MkIa and the Mk III; I suppose our priorities in conversations sounded unusual as flying talk held a much higher priority than discussions about members of the opposite sex. We laughed watching films of early Spitfires weaving their way into the sky after take off; we had both flown the Mk I which was designed without the hydraulic system that was included in the design of all later models. The Mk I retraction and extension of the undercarriage was accomplished by making twelve strokes up and down on a lever located on the right-hand side of the cockpit. As the pilot moved his right hand up and down in the pumping action the movement transferred a slight forward and backward motion to his other hand holding the control column which in turn controlled the pitch of the aeroplane. This imparted a weaving up and down motion to the flight path of the aircraft as the undercarriage was retracted, which we both found humorous (I think at this point we were becoming snobs). Jack and I felt just a little touch of superiority in having found that by locking the left forearm against the left knee while retracting the undercarriage prevented the slight forward and backward tendency of the left hand and made the climb out as it should be – smooth.

Though avoiding conscription into the Army had brought me to the point that there was a strong possibility of direct contact with the enemy, it left me with a feeling of guilt that seeking a nice secure job sweeping out hangars was rather like expecting others to perform the essential job of fighting the war, whether on land, sea or in the air. On the other hand only a few of those conscripted into the Army, Navy or Royal Air Force would actually be called upon to face the enemy directly, the vast majority surely being assigned to the essential work providing the logistics necessary to support those in actual combat; so even performing the task of sweeping out hangars, although a relatively safe job, was still supporting the war effort. At war's end I would still have been considered a serviceman who had honourably served his country, receive a pat on the back and have a joyous welcome home.

I also mused that probably the majority of people, both men and women, accepted being conscripted and were relatively happy if they were accepted into the service of their choice. It also seemed likely that a fairly large percentage would find that service life provided an element of adventure and a welcome change from the monotony of the civilian life that so many had led. Only a small percentage of those conscripted into the various services would be subjected to more danger than the Luftwaffe had already subjected them to in the bombing raids anyway. Conscientious objectors, whose pacifist views I understood and indeed shared myself, also contributed to the war effort in the work to which they were directed, but most people considered them to be of a cowardly nature, whether true or not. Although surely no one could seriously want to fight, cowardice was the general assumption that was held of conscientious objectors by some. But when the chips are down, it becomes necessary to defend those who are unable to defend themselves. Despite these thoughts and doubts about myself or of my own bravery, or lack of it, I realised that I had been accompanied by danger during all the training period and had survived the statistics that suggested that the percentage of casualties during training actually exceeded the number of casualties that aircrew received in action; of course, convincing myself of this was not easy. Being able to defend yourself or being armed to attack the enemy made some kind of sense but I was now facing the prospect of flying an unarmed aircraft in broad daylight deep into enemy territory where Bf 109s and Fw 190s of the Luftwaffe ruled the skies. By continuing on this path, was I committing suicide? Or had I just got myself inextricably in over my head? Perhaps the two-week leave that was granted would help relieve my headache. With all this justification of not needing to be in the position of not having to face the enemy, why had I got myself into where I would? Because I wanted to fly – and I love it!

For two weeks the future did not matter. Arriving home in Leicester, my mother informed me that my brother who was now in India had written home and was well, although he could give no information on exactly where he was or what he was doing. I sensed the concern Mother had for the safety of both my brother and I, which was only natural, of course, but it was a matter of concern to me. She had known at first hand the grief that accompanies war. The German bombing persisted, and the long list of military and civilian casualties was now including people close to home. My sister Edna's husband Harry had been called up, and inducted into the Royal Air Force. Although a fine person, he was very quiet and inoffensive, not the sort of person who would stand out in a crowd. He could not drive when conscripted into the RAF and it came as quite a surprise to hear that he was being trained as a driver, but why be surprised? I could not fly an aeroplane when I joined the RAF either, but this was the pattern of things in those days.

I was happy when one of the 'Three Caballeros' turned up on leave. By a coincidence that lasted for most of the war: you could almost guarantee that when one showed up the other two would also arrive momentarily. Right on time, Sid Johnson and Tony Scott arrived home on leave. Sid Johnson, his sister and parents lived on Penrith Road just around the corner from my home on Shetland Road and Tony Scott lived with his mother and sister on Doncaster Road. I was impressed that Tony's mother had at one time been engaged to the famous moving picture star Charles Laughton though the engagement never came to anything. Sid was now a member of the Glider Pilot Regiment with 6th Airborne Division and wore the wings of a glider pilot while Tony was a first mate on an Anglo-American oil tanker plying between North American ports and Britain, bringing the essential oil products necessary for the continuation of the war. As usual we had a great time, leaving the war behind and attending dances at the Palais de Dance in Humberstone Gate, the Corn Exchange in the market place and even the Grand Hotel Ballroom on London Road. I now owned a Morris Ten (10 horse power) car and managed to wangle enough black-market petrol to last out our leave and a good time was had by all.

Chapter 7

The Reaper Beckons

When anyone became aware that you flew Spitfires they would always ask, 'how many Germans have you shot down', it was embarrassing to inform them that it was a little difficult to do as there were no guns in our Spitfires. That did tend to detract from any brave image you might have held.

A spy in the sky played a much different role than that played by what a traditional spy was imagined to be, an agent hiding behind an identity that concealed his subversive gathering of intelligence; his danger lay in having his cover blown. At least the agent was safe until such time, but a spy in the sky had no cover; it was already blown as he was in plain sight at all times in a merciless environment. A target with no protection, his only hope was to be lucky enough to be able to outmanoeuvre the enemy and escape into cloud – if there were any. Flying in a predictable environment carrying guns was dangerous enough, but flying into unknown dangers over enemy territory in an aircraft without any defence did appear to make a future somewhat questionable; perhaps limited would be a more correct term, but it was the only way to obtain the intelligence needed to successfully lead to victory.

Sergeant Dearden and I reported for duty in an operational squadron at No. 1 Photographic Reconnaissance Unit headquarters at RAF Station Benson, Oxfordshire. I found my way there by taking the train to Oxford and getting a lift in a Post Office van that dropped me off close to Benson in the town of Wallingford. It was late in the evening and, not without difficulty, I stumbled in the dark to the guard room of the airfield; it was a considerable distance and, it being late, there was no one around to help me with directions. Being a 'qualified navigator' was of no help at all. Finding RAF Benson in the blackout in the unknown countryside showed what guesswork and a lot of luck could do. I slept for a few hours in the sergeants' quarters, but I still felt tired when I went to breakfast in the senior NCOs' mess, more commonly known as the sergeants' mess. Sergeant Dearden must have found a short cut as he was already there. After breakfast we reported to the commanding officer of 543 Photographic Reconnaissance Squadron in his office on the first floor of one of the hangars.

Squadron Leader Robertson seemed less than overjoyed to have two non-commissioned pilots assigned to his squadron, but welcomed us anyway. One of his first questions was if either of us wanted to go overseas. Jack replied yes, but not until after Christmas. On the other hand I declined as I had no desire to go overseas since my wish was to operate over Northern Europe where I felt I belonged. Flying from Benson would also allow me to return home every few weeks; in any case I felt that if I was to face the enemy it should be over the continent of Europe from where the attacks on Britain came. It was now autumn and it seemed to be a safe assumption that any posting overseas would be not be likely until after Christmas, which was just a few weeks away, and having observed the wheels of bureaucracy I knew they turned extremely slowly. But this was still October and the threat of any overseas posting for Jack would still be in the distant future.

After three flights to gain familiarisation with the area, I was on my way to flight dispersal after breakfast when the flight commander came from behind and laid a hand on my shoulder and said 'we have an operation for you today' – the time to pay the piper had arrived; the hooded man with the scythe was beckoning – and it was only last year I thought that by joining the RAF I would have a nice safe job and be able to sit out the war safely. Oh, what have I done? Instead of a nice safe job sweeping out hangars, I am now facing the possibility of exposing myself to the enemy and becoming a target and it somehow fails to fill me with patriotic fervour; even conscription into the Army now looked as if it might have provided more of a future than the one I was afraid I might no longer have. But it was now too late for these thoughts. The Grim Reaper with an 'I've got you now' look was probably gloating as he waited for me. I admit I was scared (no, make that *terrified*). I went to briefing and was given instructions to fly at 30,000 feet and photograph the ports of Flushing and Rotterdam. After the briefing by one of the Hornby twins (of Hornby model trains fame), who were intelligence officers at Benson, I plotted my course in pencil on a map that I still have in my possession. The Spitfire I was assigned was a Mk IV with two Williamson 36-inch focal-length cameras mounted in tandem in the fuselage behind the pilot's cockpit and no radio. The aircraft had no camouflage and was painted entirely in azure blue to make it less visible against the blue of the sky and the usual RAF insignia on the sides of the fuselage and wings were replaced with just a red circle inside a dark blue one (notice how I replaced 'target' with 'insignia'; I didn't want to be a target). The aircraft on walk-round inspection appeared to be in good condition and I could find no fault to, hopefully, have the operation scrubbed. Feeling like a condemned man walking to the scaffold, I climbed into the cockpit, fastened the parachute harness and Sutton harness, closed the side panel and, feeling somewhat less than happy, shouted 'clear' and started the engine. There was now no way that I could avoid the possibility of being shot at if the Germans chose so to do. After going through the pre-flight checks, I committed myself to flight. The sky was clear as I climbed to altitude. Off to the right the English Channel looked narrow enough to build a bridge across but, as I approached the Dutch coast, all I observed was a vast layer of low-lying stratus cloud that stretched inland as far as the eye could see. All I could do after I had reached the assigned altitude was to fly a dead-reckoning course and hopefully find holes in the cloud, although secretly I felt scared that I might see the ground and hoped that I wouldn't. My wishes were granted; I did not find any holes in the cloud. Even the dreaded Bf 109s or Fw 190s did not come up to use me for target practice, and I was terrified that they might. Having dutifully flown the route over the targets, even if it was by using dead-reckoning navigation and my Dalton computer to plot the course, after flying over where I calculated Flushing and Rotterdam to be, and having cheated death, I turned for home and with a big sigh of relief started my descent. After landing back at Benson I was driven to the debriefing room and given a small tin of fruit juice before I spilled the beans and told them everything that I had observed: nothing – nothing but cloud – although in its own small way this was first-hand information. Although this operation certainly could not be described as a display of bravery, in fact it was so bad that even the Grim Reaper had turned his head away in disdain. Having survived an operation over enemy-held territory, I had reached a status that, whatever else might be said about me, put me in an elite category, although in this case only slightly 'elite'. I was rewarded with an operational meal consisting of scarce bacon, eggs, fried tomatoes, sausage, fried potatoes, toast and, of course, tea – an odd meal for that time of day but don't look a gift horse in the mouth; I was still here to enjoy it. In fact, I even felt slightly better about myself and flying across the North Sea had lent authenticity to the ditty written in 1941 by a photographic reconnaissance pilot named Pat Bonner titled 'Tale of The PRU' that went as follows:

THE REAPER BECKONS

When you're five miles up in the heavens,
That's a hell of a lonely spot,
And its thirty degrees below zero,
Which isn't exactly hot,
And you're frozen blue like your Spitfire
And scared a Mosquito pink and
You're a thousand miles from nowhere
And there's nothing below but the drink,
It's then you'll see the Gremlins,
Green ones, gamboges and gold,
Male, female and neuter,
Gremlins both young and old,
It's no good trying to dodge them,
The lessons you learned on the link
Won't help you evade a Gremlin,
Though you boost and you jive and you jink,
White ones will wiggle your wingtips,
Male ones will muddle your maps,
Green ones will guzzle your Glycol,
Females will flutter your flaps,
Pink ones will perch on your Perspex,
And dance pirouettes on your prop,
There's a spherical, middle-aged Gremlin
Who'll spin on your stick like a top.
They'll freeze up your camera shutters,
They'll bite through your aileron wires,
They'll break and they'll bend and they'll batter,
They'll insert toasting forks in your tyres,
That is the tale of the Gremlins,
Told by the P.R.U.
(P)retty (R)uddy (U)likely to many,
but fact, none the less, to the few.

I could identify with the loneliness, although it was not until later that I would become acquainted with the Gremlins (intimately acquainted).

Flying activities continued and the number of operations from which the pilots did not return occurred with alarming frequency. Additionally, pilots had been lost in crashes while flying in bad weather and poor visibility. For the next two weeks after my first operational sortie I just flew around locally, becoming more familiar with the surrounding countryside. Skip Lewis, who was formating on me, took pictures of my Spitfire, X4786, from his Spitfire, which was equipped with an oblique camera (a 24-inch focal-length camera mounted in the upper part of the fuselage and pointed to the side) which enabled photographs to be taken of objects on that side. Skip took two pictures of my aircraft, one of which appeared in a book about Spitfires. Sergeant Lewis, although British, was said to have been a 'Clapper Boy' in the Hollywood movie industry and had returned to Britain at the start of the war to join the RAF.

It was not long before I was assigned another operation in which I was briefed to take photographs of the ports of Dunkirk, Ostend and Flushing on the French and Belgian coasts. The trip was uneventful. Although the possibility of enemy fighters was nonetheless scary, I felt that being a little scared (although terrified was more appropriate) was to some extent excusable; after all I was piloting an unarmed aircraft in broad daylight in places where Luftwaffe fighters roamed. As I returned it was the balloon barrage over London shrouded in a thick yellow London fog that presented the greatest threat. Heading home in a westerly direction north of London I was shocked as a barrage balloon suddenly loomed above me. Right away I knew I was in the wrong place and immediately climbed to an altitude that would take me higher than the balloons, hoping I would not hit one of their threatening cables as I climbed. Resorting to seeking navigational assistance on my radio (a VHF which was far more effective than the earlier TR9 radios) I requested a QDM (Magnetic Course for Base), but received no reply. In the extremely limited visibility of the fog I flew on a course to the north to avoid any further possibility of confrontation with balloon cables and tried again to obtain a QDM. This time I raised a reply and was given a course. Although it did not coincide with the direction I knew Benson to be in I followed the instructions. When I was informed that I was over my base, I could see that it was not Benson and told them that this was not my base; I was then told to land to find out where I was. After landing, I asked the name and location of this aerodrome and was informed that it was RAF Station Radlett, located several miles north of London. With that information I curtly stated 'Operational PRU' and took off again and found my own way back to Benson. So much for radio navigational aids, but it had enabled me to determine my exact location for which I was grateful in that miserable visibility.

It should not have come as a surprise that, while on Christmas leave, it was I, not Sergeant Dearden, who received a notice to report back to Benson for immediate posting overseas. I was a slow learner; I had been told time and time again that if you wanted a posting close to home volunteer for an assignment that was as far away as possible. So it was predictable that Jack, having volunteered for an overseas posting and I having stated that I did not want to go overseas, it would be me who would be recalled from Christmas leave the day before Christmas for immediate posting overseas. But, of course, immediate did not mean today, tomorrow or even next week. I supposed they possibly were transferring me away because my performance was less than that desired, despite having covered every target as ordered, but was it really necessary to recall me from Christmas leave and then take no action? But it could have been in connection with Operation TORCH that was in progress as the Allies invaded French North-West Africa, but if that were so the only danger I could present to the enemy would be to throw my Dalton computer at them. The Dalton computer was just a circular calculator with a frosted panel on which course calculations could be made in pencil; it was also used to make other calculations such as true speed and altitude determinations. The device was small and was strapped to the pilot's thigh above the knee; with that as my main armament I could hardly imagine that the Germans would shrink from me in blind terror. A few more days elapsed and, still not having been sent overseas, I was assigned another operation photographing German airfields and landing grounds around the European towns of Ostend, Bruges, Ghent and Zeebrugge. Although still apprehensive, but now it only took the form of being tense, I had a feeling of gratification that I had tested myself and found I was not lacking – just stupid for being psychologically unprepared to face this type of danger in the first place. However, I realised that probably the only way to cope was by getting used to the danger in the same way I had become used to the bombs falling during Luftwaffe attacks; you just get used to the danger and I found fear was reduced to a manageable tenseness.

True to form, authority exerted itself a few days later when, together with four other non-commissioned pilots from the other two squadrons based at Benson, I was told to pack my things and was sent to a transit unit in Scotland. There we five were issued with tropical uniforms. Armed with this information and with our newly-acquired knowledge of how the logic of bureaucracy worked, we were able to deduce that our destination would be located somewhere in the Arctic. After reaching Gourock by train the five of us were embarked aboard the *Letitia*, a former armed merchant vessel being used as a troopship. We were overwhelmed by the luxury of our shipboard accommodation which consisted of a mess deck with a sign stencilled on the bulkhead designating the area as providing space for 186 occupants. Unfortunately, someone apparently was unable to count since the number of personnel assigned to the black hole of *Letitia* somewhat exceeded that number by at least 100 per cent. There were hammocks strung from bulkhead to bulkhead and after all the hammocks were filled, personnel (the troops) had to sleep on the mess tables, on the deck, and literally on top of each other. The dining salon for we NCOs, if one may be excused for referring to it in such a gracious manner, was a small compartment reserved for senior non-commissioned officers; it left much to be desired but the food was great and included items such as steak and other almost forgotten luxury items. This at least provided a respite from the cattle-car atmosphere of the black hole where the unfortunate masses were fed. NCOs even had a recreational area provided for them, a place where they could play cards, read books or engage in whatever other acceptable activities would enable them to pass the time away, but I was unable to understand how those poor unfortunate dwellers in the black hole could tolerate eating and sleeping in that intolerable atmosphere.

After sailing down the Clyde and heading in God knows what direction, the weather was not only overcast but the visibility was reduced to just a few hundred yards. The *Letitia* was joined by other vessels and formed into a convoy that included an aircraft carrier of the Royal Navy named HMS *Argus*. It was rumoured to be a ship left over from the Great War and was nicknamed the *Flatiron*. With its complement of old Swordfish biplanes it made us feel that we had been abandoned and were probably being offered to the enemy as a sacrifice. That being as it may, it paled into insignificance when we started to experience rough seas; the sea became not just ruffled, it became downright angry. Later it proved that we were crossing the Bay of Biscay and that was not, and is still not, noted as an area where calm seas prevail. In the NCOs' recreational area the atmosphere took on the form of a gymnasium, with exercises including avoiding tables and chairs as they slid, although some say 'flew', from one side of the area to the other; it was challenging to maintain an upright posture without having something to hold on to. The black hole of the accommodation deck became untenable as the poor unfortunates lost control of their stomachs, creating an atmosphere that could no longer be tolerated by the five of us. We had no alternative but to sleep on deck and pity the poor souls who had to endure that wretched atmosphere below. Despite the overwhelming seasickness that prevailed, it did not affect the five of us; as pilots our stomachs were used to motion when flying and seasickness did not affect us. One morning when the five of us sat down for breakfast there was only one other person in attendance, an army sergeant major. Sergeant Fletcher, of course, had to be a wag and said, 'What I would like for breakfast is a nice, big, greasy, pork chop.' With that the sergeant major turned a pale shade of green and the party of six was reduced to a party of five. The sea calmed, and the temperature became quite pleasant, making us wonder which way we were going to the Arctic, but, with a brightly lit horizon together with small fishing boats displaying masthead lights and our being able to see the stars, we thought it was probably Lisbon and that we might be on our way to support Operation TORCH and join the invasion of North West Africa. The question now was exactly where are we heading?

Having checked the time as the strokes of Big Ben were heard on the BBC when the 9 o'clock news was broadcast over the loudspeaker system, we unanimously decided that Big Ben was three seconds slow. We knew that was not possible and were amazed at the end of the news broadcast when the BBC announcer apologised for Big Ben being three seconds slow – the British Empire must be disintegrating. But any conjecture as to how that could have happened was interrupted by an Australian sergeant pilot by the name of Keith Campbell who said 'Funny if this was loaded' as he picked up a service issue Smith and Wesson .38 calibre police special revolver. It was; the bullet entered the composite deck, travelled under the other four pilots, emerging beyond them and splattered itself against the steel bulkhead. But all good things must come to an end: when the slave (excuse me) troop ship rounded Point Europa, we knew that our destination was Gibraltar.

The harbour at Gibraltar was crowded with shipping. We spent the night aboard before disembarking but the information that a two-man submarine from Algeciras was sinking Allied shipping in the harbour did not provide for a good night's rest. But this was not the Arctic; this was the warm hive of activity that was Gibraltar, where both sides of a long wide runway that protruded out into the Bay of Algeciras were filled with aircraft being assembled. The main street was full of shops overflowing with goods that had not been seen in Britain since the start of the war. It also seemed that every shop was bordered by a bar on either side filled with servicemen from many nations. Walking around the casemates certainly provided the atmosphere of the Rock being an outpost of Empire; the view across the Straits of Gibraltar, together with the huge guns pointing out into and across the straits toward North Africa, certainly provided the Rock with an impressive command of the entrance to the Mediterranean. Exploring the town, I found a small cemetery just off the main street containing the graves of a number of sailors dating back to the time of the Battle of Trafalgar. It was a surprise that these sailors had not died in the battle; according to the epitaphs they had succumbed to an epidemic of cholera.

It seemed that everything that was unattainable in England was available in profusion – bananas, watches, liqueur, cigarettes and jewellery, just to mention a few of the items. The Bristol Hotel had been requisitioned to accommodate members of His Majesty's Forces; in the bar a Tom Collins cost just sixpence (2.5p). Although I neither drank nor smoked, I noticed that cigarettes, which were so scarce in Britain, were available in abundance and cost only one shilling and a penny (just over 5p) for fifty.

Shortly after arriving, and while waiting for information as to what our fate would be, we were told that our aircraft had been destroyed in a bombing raid and, because there were no aircraft for us to fly, we would be returned to Great Britain – on the same ship on which we had just arrived. I figured that having been put to all this trouble there had to be some compensatory way of making up for it. I had no trouble in identifying that there were easy profits to be made by taking back something that was not readily obtainable in Britain and taking such items back could be profitable; in any case cigarettes would provide an uplift for a few smokers in the stringent conditions that prevailed there. Although I would have loved to take back some watches that were so sorely needed, with so little money all I could afford were cigarettes, so I bought 1,000 Senior Service cigarettes in tins called flat fifties and stuffed them in my kitbag ready to board the *Letitia* when ordered. While waiting I was amused and for that matter surprised by the behaviour displayed by the mix of military personnel both in the bars and outside on the main street. I saw drunken soldiers fighting each other over which was better, Scotland or Scotland, and wondered why drink would cause them to be fighting each other over what appeared to me to be the same thing or, for that matter, why, if they really wanted to fight, not save it for the enemy. But I realised that these servicemen in many different branches of the services were certainly stressed by being snatched away from what may have been a monotonous and perhaps unrewarding life and were now propelled into an environment that was unknown, exciting, and difficult to understand, although the discipline of military life had turned them into a cohesive body of men who would later prove themselves in battle against the enemy. Admirable, but it was not the sort of service life that conscription into the Army might have entailed and it had no appeal for me; it was now more indelibly impressed on my mind that joining the

Royal Air Force had been the right decision. After the ship was re-supplied and the five of us were back on board, the cabins we had been promised to compensate for the miserable overloading on the outbound trip if we should happen to be on the return voyage were just that – a promise, a false one. If nothing else, there were relatively few passengers on the return trip, making it a far less uncomfortable voyage than the one to Gibraltar. The enjoyment of being reprieved from a permanent posting overseas and returning to Britain had the gloss taken off by a young pilot officer of the Royal Air Force, who did not wear any badge that would identify him as being an aircrew member, taking it upon himself to volunteer the services of the five of us to man the gun turrets of the troopship, stating that these men are trained in the use of guns. That may have been true, but they had trained gunners to man the turrets and we were told that under no circumstances were we to fire the guns if enemy aircraft attacked; we were to wait until the gunners came and took over. We were beginning to get the idea that if a mere pilot officer, who had probably been a clerk a few weeks before, could be so stupid, the country was in real trouble. As trained pilots who not only knew how to fire the guns, but were also experts in aircraft recognition, being told not to fire the guns if we were attacked made it appear that the officer had only done this either to show his 'superiority' or for some unknown reason to punish the five of us; either that or he was a secret German agent who wanted to get the ship sunk. We spent this luxurious return cruise manning the gun turrets four hours on and four hours off all the way from Gibraltar to Glasgow. While we were manning the gun turrets we figured that the regular gunners were probably laughing their heads off in their quarters. Fortunately we were not attacked or we would have faced a court martial for disobeying orders but, if nothing else, we were rewarded with wonderful views from the gun turrets as we sailed up the Clyde to dock at Gourock. Our view of officers was eroded from the demi-gods that we once thought they might be and we were disappointed that the pilot officer did not fall overboard and have to swim home.

You can see what fun we were having making our contribution to the war effort, and the people who were making all this possible were being paid for it.

One thing I had done right was to bring back two huge stalks of bananas from Gibraltar. Bananas had not been seen in the UK since the start of the war and HM Customs and Excise raised no objections, but they did query the cigarettes when I told them I had 1,000 Senior Service cigarettes. The customs officer replied, 'Oh well, you will smoke nine hundred and eighty before you go ashore won't you?' To me it did seem odd to be depriving the British public of comforts that might provide some relief from the stress they were under but I rationalised it with the thought that such comforts were probably in such short supply that it was better to make them available for the troops overseas who were probably under greater stress; that would make more sense. Our arrival on Sauchiehall Street in Glasgow presented an interesting sight; I was carrying the two huge stalks of bananas hanging around my neck while each of my four travelling companions kept the bananas safe from being plundered by anyone who still remembered what bananas were. We were armed with our Smith and Wesson revolvers although, of course, there was no threat; but the five of us must have appeared to be a humorous sight – 'bananas with an armed guard' even though our guns were in their holsters.

After a week's leave and distributing bananas to friends, relatives and a facility that provided good deeds to local medical facilities, I purveyed the cigarettes to smokers showing withdrawal symptoms. I must have been getting soft, although I could have sold them for what they were sold for in the shops. Realising the stress that everyone was under with the increasing pressures of war together with the continuing bombing attacks I sold them at a price a little more than what I had paid for them – but I had not become too soft. I had made a profit – probably enough for a beer.

Reporting back to No.1 PRU at Benson, I was assigned to 541 Squadron (543 Squadron had been disbanded, possibly due to there being no pilots left). Sergeant Dearden and I were the only remaining pilots of what had been B Flight, but before recommencing operational flying I was instructed to go to Gillingham in Kent for an interview. I arrived in Gillingham and was escorted into a tunnel that led deep underground where I was told that this was the headquarters of No. 17 Group RAF. The reason for the visit was for an interview to determine if I was suitable material to be commissioned as an officer. I wondered if the world had abandoned what little sanity it might have retained. I found it well nigh impossible to believe that submitting the RAF Form 1020a while at No. 8 OTU in Fraserburgh could have triggered such an action, but wonders never cease and perhaps miracles did happen. On the other hand, even though I had now perfected the speech and mannerisms of the so called 'upper class', I knew that a commissioning interview would be fruitless, knowing that they would never allow anyone with a background and reputation like mine to become a commissioned officer. When asked what difference I thought there would be between the duties of my present rank and that of an officer, I replied 'Very little,' as I would fly just the same operations and continue to help the men of lower rank in solving their problems, cutting passes, listening to complaints etc. The air officer conducting the interview replied, 'Yes, an officer's first duty is the welfare of his men.' At that I left the interview thinking that many of the officers that I had experienced in the past had apparently been unaware of what their first duty was. Since my duties as a sergeant appeared to be identical to those of an officer, the only change would be in pay and prestige, so what would be the point in enrolling me as an officer in the RAF? I dismissed the matter from my mind as just another wasted exercise.

As I returned to Benson I wondered what had triggered this turn of events. I remembered that when Jacky and I had joined 543 Squadron the commander had asked, among other things, why we would want to be commissioned. I had dismissed the question from my mind, thinking that he probably preferred to have only officers on the squadron. The only reason that I could think of on the spur of the moment was that the sandpaper-like serge from which the enlisted men's uniforms were made caused a sore neck while an officer's uniform was made from much smoother material and would not be as rough on the neck when constantly scanning for enemy aircraft. It was probably the wrong thing to have said but I had been more concerned with the apprehension about what operations against the enemy could entail. Heck, I was a pilot, not a social climber.

A Flight of 541 Squadron, to which I was now attached, had been moved to a satellite airfield at Mount Farm, twelve miles in the direction of Oxford from Benson. There was little there but runways; our living quarters were maintained at Benson where Jacky Dearden and I had rooms in the sergeants' quarters. This arrangement necessitated our being driven back and forth to Mount Farm each day in a Humber station-wagon. The driver was a pretty WAAF who made the ride a welcome change from the two-mile bicycle ride to dispersal as we had done previously at Benson. Apart from the runways, Mount Farm had very little else, a few huts and Spam sandwiches for lunch and these did not taste too good due to the overwhelming smells from the surrounding farms. The next few days at Mount Farm were occupied by making two or three local flights, which was a rather pleasant way of spending time in the prevailing warm weather. This brief interlude ended abruptly when the flight commander told me to report to briefing. Having covered targets previously on the French and Belgian coasts, I did not have quite as many butterflies in my stomach as I previously had, although apprehension was still a better word; but it was not as scary as it used to be.

The operation called for photographing various targets among which were airfields and the ports of Cherbourg and Le Havre. I was assigned a Spitfire Mk XI for this sortie. The Mk XI was the latest and most up-to-date photographic reconnaissance aircraft at the time and was considerably different from the earlier types that I had flown. The Spitfires I had flown at No. 8 OTU were mostly early fighter models with eight Browning .303 machine guns mounted in the wings and thick bulletproof windscreens and had a tiny rear-view mirror mounted on the top of the canopy. When the throttle was opened, these docile aircraft would joyfully waggle their tails as if in anticipation of the take off. The Mk IV photographic Spitfires that I had been flying since joining PRU were much heavier than the fighters; their wing leading edges had been redesigned as fuel tanks and held petrol instead of guns. The main fuel tank mounted in the fuselage between the engine and the cockpit held 86 gallons and the two wing tanks held 66 gallons each, providing a total fuel capacity of more than 218 gallons, enough to be able to stay in the air for as long as six hours and provide a range of several hundred miles. The Spitfires designed for photographic reconnaissance had a moulded windscreen and two rear-view mirrors mounted in bubbles moulded into each side of the sliding canopy. Although those mirrors would be handy to see an enemy fighter on your tail as it was about to shoot you out of the sky, the real purpose was to recognise a condensation trail if one was forming. Such a trail would provide the enemy with your exact position and, if that happened, it was a good idea to change altitude and direction and stop the condensation trail from forming to prevent you being used for target practice by the German anti-aircraft gunners. Another use of the mirrors was to avoid anti-aircraft fire attempting to straddle the path of your aircraft with bursts initiated from behind; as the bursts came close it was a good time to make a rapid change of course and altitude before shrapnel from them came close enough to be dangerous. The heavy PRU aeroplanes were fitted with either 24-inch or 36-inch focal-length cameras mounted in tandem in the fuselage behind the pilot's cockpit. Due to the mounting of the cameras, this required that the aircraft not be subjected to negative G forces (a restriction that applied to all high-level PRU aircraft). Despite the restrictions they still handled well, although the aileron control (used to keep the wings level) was somewhat heavier than the fighter models. The Spitfire Mk XI, however, was a much heavier aircraft than the earlier PR Spitfires and weighed almost twice the weight of the original Spitfire prototype that bore the number K5054, which was parked outside one of the hangars at Benson. A larger, more advanced, Merlin engine powered the Mk XI; it incorporated a two-stage supercharger that provided as much engine boost pressure (power) at 21,000 feet as at ground level and the engine nacelle was a foot longer to accommodate an engine much larger than on previous models. It also required added procedures in flight; my reaction to being assigned this strange aircraft that was so much heavier, with a much longer nose and a two-stage supercharger, caused me to point out to the flight commander that I had never flown this model before. The flight commander replied, 'Well now's the chance to learn.' Of course, I would fly it, but I would have liked to have had the opportunity to acquaint myself with its handling characteristics with a familiarisation flight before trying to feel them out in the unfriendly skies over enemy territory. The added operating instructions included one for the engine 'boost controller' that was to be set in the 'normal' position for take off; after climbing to an altitude in excess of 21,000 feet, the pilot was to throttle back fully and switch the boost control to the 'auto' setting before opening the throttle to the desired power setting. The procedure was to be reversed before descending below 21,000 feet. I thought this is all very well, but it puts me at a disadvantage in the event of being intercepted in an aircraft that is strange to me, but I had been sweet talked that, in the event of an interception at high altitude, the aircraft could climb faster than enemy fighters thus enabling the threat to be neutralised. Being told that did not prove that it was really so. Feeling less than happy, there was no option but to obey orders and fly the sortie. After accomplishing the walk-round inspection and finding everything in order, I climbed into the cockpit and fastened my parachute and Sutton harnesses and went through the start-up procedure. After the uneventful engine run up and all the pre-flight checks proving to be satisfactory, I started to taxi to the runway and noted that the aeroplane moved in a very sluggish, down in the mouth, manner as it lumbered to the take-off position. Having checked that everything was satisfactory, I completed the vital actions before take off and advanced the throttle. I immediately noticed that, as the machine lumbered forward, it had a very marked tendency to swing due to the torque of the 1,500hp engine and, although I had no difficulty in correcting it with rudder, I thought this could be a big problem on a short runway where it would be necessary to open the throttle rapidly to full power. The runway at Mount Farm was long and as the aircraft broke ground I was pleased that at least it felt solid. I started the climb toward the south coast and the English Channel and made a fix to determine my position before setting out across the Channel to France.

The aircraft climbed rapidly and as the altitude increased I was happy to find that the ailerons on this model were once again light and that the controls were balanced the same as I had experienced on the early fighters I had originally flown. The aileron controls on photographic aircraft had become much heavier, probably due to the weight of the petrol carried in the wing leading edges and it was pleasant to once again feel nicely balanced controls. As I climbed, I was getting the feel of this heavy aeroplane and felt comfortable with the way it handled and less apprehensive about flying it over the enemy-held territory around Cherbourg. This improvement in my feeling of security, if that is the right word, was shattered when the engine suddenly went berserk and tried to tear itself out of the airframe. Realising that the engine and aeroplane were still in one piece, I regained control, wondering what had happened; it was then that I remembered that I had not included in the vital actions before take off to set the 'boost controller' to the 'normal' position and the supercharger, being programmed with the control set in the 'auto' position, automatically switched to high speed at 21,000 feet. It had suddenly increased the boost pressure from a minus value to a positive boost pressure of 18 inches of mercury, providing the same amount of power at that altitude as the engine would have had at ground level. This sudden increase of the air-manifold pressure to the engine had the effect of providing so much torque that it twisted the engine in its mount so much that I thought that it was going to tear loose from the airframe. Making a mistake is human but with an aircraft it can be fatal, so I indelibly wrote in my mind not to make the same mistake again. But I was over enemy territory and any feeling of invulnerability that I might have had was not helped by what had happened and the most dangerous part of the operation was still ahead: I had yet to photograph all the targets before I might be safe.

The Luftwaffe appeared to ignore me, for which I was grateful and, after completing coverage of the targets, I still had not seen any sign of an interception. Before the Germans could change their minds, I crossed my fingers and with a feeling of relief turned north to high tail it back towards the English Channel and start my descent. Apparently, I had become complacent again and to keep my nerves on edge as I started my descent I completely forgot about the automatic 'boost control' – again! After the relief of not being intercepted and breathing a sigh of relief, I now had my nerves shattered by making the same mistake I had made as I climbed to altitude and scared myself out of my wits; this time I had forgotten to throttle back and switch the boost control to 'normal' before I descended through 21,000 feet, so the same thing happened again, but this time in reverse: once again the engine tried to tear itself out of the airframe, scaring the living daylights out of me, but this time it felt as though the brakes had been slammed on. To put it mildly, I was more shaken by this than I would have been by a possible interception. I began to wonder if there might have been some merit in having a nice safe job sweeping out hangars. But, with shaken nerves, I arrived back safely at Mount Farm and, after making a good landing, remembered the flight commander's words, 'Well now's the chance to learn', and thought to myself 'But not like that – isn't there an easier way to learn?', especially when you are over enemy territory.

After a day or two of familiarising myself with the Spitfire Mk XI and having the freedom to enjoy myself flying around the English countryside, I was assigned to photograph an area around Caen in northern France and now, had gained more confidence, that is if you can term it confidence when you are flying an unarmed aircraft over enemy territory in broad daylight – some might term it stupidity or downright insane, but nonetheless a dirty job that somebody had to do. The operation was unremarkable; I covered the targets and returned to base happy that the Luftwaffe had apparently not shown even the slightest interest in me.

For the next few days I was occupied in familiarisation flights with the Mk XI that included an operational flight over Dieppe and continuing inland into France as far as Compiègne. No enemy aircraft showed up, causing me to wonder why such heavy losses had occurred at the time of my joining PRU at Benson. In the middle of March I flew an operation to targets in and around Paris, the Renault works at Billancourt and the aerodrome at Villacoublay. The Germans were using Villacoublay as a repair base for the Fw 190 fighter, an aircraft to be avoided whenever possible. There were no problems or any objections from fighter aircraft of the Luftwaffe on this operation either, but I was disappointed I was unable to spot the Eiffel Tower.

An operation to cover targets around Cherbourg, Dieppe and Caen was flown by an American pilot in the RAF by the name of Bob Luepke, a sergeant pilot who was awaiting transfer to the USAAF; it was his first sortie and he had wanted to fly an operation before his transfer to the US forces. Bob was intercepted while covering the target at Cherbourg and managed to escape by fleeing. Sadly, he made the mistake of going back to try and complete coverage of the target. The Luftwaffe was waiting; he was shot down and killed.

You know the enemy is looking for you, but what do you do
when he finds you?

I was assigned to fly an operation shortly afterwards to cover targets in the same area where Bob Luepke had been shot down and I was determined not to make any mistake that could result in an ending such as happened to Bob, but I was still apprehensive about the exposure. After covering many of the targets I was feeling more confident and was not too concerned about the messages I was receiving on the radio giving me courses to fly. I assumed that this was some sort of game the Germans were playing in an attempt to lead me into a trap, but then the radio became full of crackling and static, but I was complacent as I only had one target left to cover before going home. I had to wait for a few minutes for a patch of cloud to move away before I could photograph the airfield at Everacy and head home across the English Channel.

While I waited the radio came to life and I received a clear message from an RAF radar tracking station in England: 'Ranger three-two, bandits at three o'clock', and then even more urgently 'Bandits attacking at three o'clock', and my callsign was – 'Ranger three-two'. The enemy fighters were attacking me from out of the sun, in my blind spot. I could not see tracer bullets, but I was not looking for them either. I could not see my attackers in my mirrors due to the sun blinding me. I felt like a sitting duck.

With visions of what had happened to Sergeant Lupke, I could not think of any defensive manoeuvre other than push the throttle wide open, put the propeller into full fine pitch and put the nose down. My only hope was that the Spitfire Mk XI with its powerful 1,500hp Merlin engine would be too fast for the enemy fighters to get close enough to hit me. The aircraft surged downward, heading due north across the English Channel. All I could do was keep my fingers crossed that cannon shells and bullets would not start breaking up my aeroplane, or me, and hoping they could not catch up with me or hit me with their guns. As I went through 24,000 feet my airspeed indicator indicated that I was flying at a speed in excess of 520 miles per hour. I was having to hold the control column with both hands and knees to maintain control. My speed was such that, from the point of interception, flying at 28,000 feet, to Mount Farm at ground level took only ten minutes. The relief of having escaped was overwhelming. I was impressed that my Spitfire had shown it could outrun the enemy aircraft. I decided the Mk XI was up to its job and, although I failed, my Spitfire hadn't.

However, I wondered what caused the buffeting as I crossed back over the English Channel; the weather over the Channel had been perfectly clear with no sign of rough air earlier. It was some years later that I first heard of

Plate 1: The student pilots at the start of advanced flying training.

Plate 2: A Tiger Moth of the type used at 21 EFTS in 1942.

Plate 3: A Miles Master MK 1 with the Kestral Engine.

Plate 4: The good guys at Chetwynd with Charlie Chan and Tich in the centre.

Plate 5: The jolly French contingent a Chetwynd.

Plate 6: Hawker Hurricane.

Plate 7: The dreaded underpowered Blackburn Botha.

Plate 8: The Westland Lysander – docile and fun to fly.

Plate 9: Squires Gate showing the long runway.

Plate 10: The Heinkel Bomber Works, north of Stettin.

Plate 11: Lubeck with bomb damage clearly visible in 1943.

Plate 12: A picture of Spitfire X4786 flown by the author in November 1942.

Plate 13: Spitfire EN 407 and I after delivery to Algiers in 1943.

Plate 14: My P38 and I at Maison Blanch 1943.

Plate 15: The 'Mudhen' at Mt. Farm after flying from Algiers 1943.

buffeting as the speed of sound was approached and, at 520 mph indicated, my air speed, when adjusted for altitude and temperature, provided a true air speed close to that. On reflection, I probably had taken the only evasive action possible as they were coming directly out of I the sun, blinding me from seeing them. Luckily, there may have been sufficient separation that they were unable to hit me, enabling me to take the evasive action that avoided me from becoming a casualty of war. Afterwards I wondered if I could have maintained better vigilance: I might have been able to see them first, but they were attacking directly out of the sun and the only way I could have any awareness of their presence was by the radio warning that had enabled me to escape. I was surprised that my reaction was not one of blind terror and I had reacted to the threat coolly and calmly; but that urgent radio warning before the enemy fighters were able to shoot me down provided me with just enough time to escape. Without that warning, oh, I don't want to think! Just another day at the office. But that was close and resolved never to let it happen again – but I did.

The Royal Air Force No. 1 Photographic Reconnaissance Unit discontinued their operations from Mount Farm and turned the field over to the United States Army Air Forces where they would operate their F-4 Lightning photographic aircraft when they arrived from the United States. Because of this the RAF operations that had been conducted at that location would again be made from Benson. On my days off at Benson I enjoyed roaming the countryside and exploring the Thames valley from Henley to Oxford. I especially enjoyed the old buildings of Marlow and the many interesting old mansions in that area of the country and particularly familiarising myself with the interface between the different branches of the RAF. I visited Bomber Command Headquarters. I was surprised to find them in a most unlikely place; Air Marshal Arthur Harris commanded the huge bomber force from a large complex constructed beneath a small unassuming house in High Wycombe. The massive destructive capability that the bombers were able to inflict on the enemy emanated from orders given under this modest little house.

I become more closely acquainted with RAF Medmenham, located in Danesfield House. Danesfield House, a beautiful mansion with Tudor chimneys and overlooking a bend of the Thames, seemed an unlikely place for an RAF activity but, despite its stately appearance, it housed a highly classified activity known as the Central Interpretation Unit (CIU). This unit interpreted and extracted intelligence from the photographic images taken by photographic-reconnaissance squadrons of the RAF and later those taken by the United States Army Air Forces' F-4s and F-5s. Observing the work at CIU, it was impressive to see the amount of intelligence being gleaned from photographs. I met Flight Officer Constance Babington Smith of the Women's Auxiliary Air Force, a highly skilled WAAF officer and leading interpreter. In her speciality of aircraft intelligence she oversaw a broad spectrum of the intelligence gathering. Just one of the many intelligence tasks was keeping track of all enemy shipping. She pointed out that intelligence enabled determination not only of where the vessels had been but also where they were going and the type of cargo they were carrying. When found to be carrying a cargo that had sufficient potential for damage to the Allies, Coastal Command or other appropriate activity would be called upon to destroy the vessel. It was not hard to see the importance of gathering intelligence, considering all of the enemy military installations, airfields, aircraft, naval vessels and military activities, not to mention keeping track of any threatening developments. Observing new technology developments, just touching on the amount of intelligence that was being extracted that aerial espionage comprised an overwhelming 80 per cent of all the intelligence that was gathered by any means. An unusual picture of what proved to be a real threat in the not too distant future was pointed out by Constance Babington Smith; it was a photograph of an aeroplane flying over the Baltic near Peenemunde. What was remarkable about this aircraft was that it did not have a propeller. It was an early V1 'buzz-bomb' with which we would become unpleasantly acquainted later when they were used to attack London and the surrounding area. This insight into the intelligence that was extracted from aerial photographs impressed me with how important my work was and made me feel that I was actively contributing to the war effort.

When asked to volunteer to join a group of photographic reconnaissance pilots that Group Captain Isherwood was assembling to operate from Russia to reach targets that could not be reached from Britain, I declined as I felt I was accomplishing what I had been trained to do by covering targets from England and had no desire to go overseas. The group did not go to Russia anyway, the reason given for the cancellation being that Russia would not permit photographic reconnaissance to operate from there because they considered us to be spies. On reflection I realised that is what we were, spies in the sky, gathering intelligence by means of aerial espionage. Although we were described by the sanitised title of photographic-reconnaissance pilots I realised that we were spies, but not of the secretive type who were only in danger when their cover was blown; we had no cover, we were in plain sight for the enemy to neutralise us if and when they could. But that was the hazard that an aerial spy had to accept when flying photographic-reconnaissance operations. Obviously my sanity had markedly deteriorated; I was beginning to enjoy what I was doing and enjoyed operating from Benson. When not on duty I spent my time enjoying the history of the surrounding countryside in Berkshire and adjacent counties. I felt at home and very fortunate to be operating from Benson.

Assigned to cover Zeebrugge, Bruges and Antwerp again, and having operated over that area a number of times, I looked upon it as being a sort of holiday as it was only along the French and Belgian coast line. I had now learned, for the moment, that interception in such areas could only be serious if you failed to see the enemy first, a lesson I had gleaned the hard way near Cherbourg. On my return to Benson, as customary I buzzed the dispersal to indicate I had film magazines to be retrieved. Becoming accustomed to, and able to live with the dangers of operational flying, my exuberance was reflected in my display as I buzzed the flight dispersal. Flying fast and low over the field directly towards the flight dispersal, I increased altitude slowly before pulling up sharply over the flight hut to reach circuit altitude; there I closed the throttle and kicked in left rudder to cause the aircraft to skid, effectively reducing my air speed to that required for undercarriage extension. After extending the undercarriage and flaps, I brought the machine down to a perfect three-point landing. At the flight dispersal I shut the engine down and watched the camera magazines being unloaded before entering the flight hut to await transportation to the post-operation interrogation office for debriefing. As I entered the hut the flight commander started chewing me out for the display I had made buzzing the airfield, even though this is what we were instructed to do. It came as a surprise when he accused me of losing control of my aeroplane. That was insulting. I knew I had performed everything in perfect safety using careful judgement. I found myself in trouble with the flight commander when he threatened to send me on a disciplinary course. Wondering if he could not recognise or know how to control an aircraft in the manner that I had just displayed, the flight commander's flying skills must have left a great deal to be desired. I summed it up by concluding that it was probably an officer having a bad day and venting his irritation on a lowly sergeant. But perhaps there were some deeper feelings that prompted the flight commander's outburst. Shortly before, a visiting squadron leader on take off had crashed the wing of his Spitfire into a flight hut after apparently imbibing too much in the officers' mess. The crash claimed the squadron leader's life together with an unfortunate member of the ground personnel, but I did not drink, or fly irresponsibly, and felt that the flight commander had no cause to vent his feelings on me. But, if that were the case, the relief of successfully returning from the danger of an operation should not have been ruined. To me that was reprehensible.

The disciplinary course did not materialise, but I did find that I had been living in a fool's paradise. This threat of being disciplined always hanging over the heads of non-commissioned pilots appeared to be overdone. A sergeant pilot by the name of Mowbray was reported by the military police (MPs) for having the top button of his uniform undone, the informal badge of a fighter pilot. As punishment he was assigned to sweep out the officers' mess like a menial servant. It seemed highly unlikely that any disciplinary action would have been taken against an officer who had failed to fasten the top button of his uniform. The risks taken in combat were identical for both commissioned and non-commissioned pilots and detailing a non-commissioned pilot to perform such a menial task as sweeping the officers' mess seemed to me humiliating and unnecessary.

But what if there is no cloud?

An operation over Holland became dangerous. As I passed over Vensendorf, just south of the Zuider Zee, I again failed to see an enemy aircraft and was intercepted. Scared out of my wits at again being jumped by an enemy aircraft and not even aware that an enemy fighter was getting close enough to attack, I instantly selected full fine pitch of the propeller and maximum boost to try to reach clouds 3,000 feet below me where I could hide, if I could dodge the enemy bullets in the meantime. This course of action was probably not the correct one, but the enemy had caught me by surprise once more and not seeing the enemy first could again have proved fatal. The attacking pilot missed me for whatever reason, but I was not an easy target as I dived for the cloud and my evasive actions made me a more difficult target to hit. It worked and I was hidden in cloud and feeling very relieved to have gotten away with it. As I descended through 18,000 feet of cloud and rain I thought that normally I would hate the challenge of this weather, but if the bad weather had not moved in I did not want to think of what might have happened. I might have avoided being shot down but now I was down to 200 feet before I broke out of the cloud over the sea. While glad that bad weather had closed in, I had no idea of where I was. Using a highly developed technique called 'guesswork', I realised that because I could not see land I was probably flying into the Thames Estuary and made a turn to the north. After a few minutes on the northern course, I turned due west, the result of my calculated navigation (intuition). I crossed the coast of Suffolk at Southwold at my designated crossing-in point, but at an altitude much less than the planned 3,000 feet. Although the cloud base was low it lifted a little over the land and I flew back to Benson with no problem thinking that I had dodged the fickle finger of fate again and wondered what the hell they were thinking when they disciplined Sergeant Mowbray for the heinous offence of having his top button undone when the next day he could be subjected to the same danger that I had just experienced? I guess hazards are not the prerogative of the Germans alone.

Within the following few days I was to have good cause to question the wisdom of avoiding conscription into the Army. Had I got myself out of the frying pan into the fire? With the April weather remaining fine with ceiling and visibility unlimited (CAVU) weather conditions, I was instructed to report for briefing for another operation. I had become used to flirting around the channel ports and the low countries and had even enjoyed trying to spot the Eiffel Tower from 30,000 feet while flying over Paris, but the next sortie would contain nothing but elements of danger and an impossible situation to overcome in order to return at all.

The following sortie seemed more like committing suicide than defending my country, I survived but my return to England was more hazardous than the sortie.

The briefing for the next operation was not for a holiday trip; it sounded more like an execution warrant. It was a maximum range sortie of approximately 900 miles, mostly over enemy territory. The targets included Stettin and Rostock, several hundred miles to the east on the far side of Germany. I nearly had a heart attack, and the targets were even farther from England than Berlin. To reach them would require flying hundreds of miles across Germany, almost to the Polish border. I took off and headed to RAF Ludham in Norfolk, near the North Sea coast, to have the fuel tanks topped off, not feeling very happy. At Ludham I would need to refuel again on my return as I would be almost out of fuel. I checked the radio en route to Ludham; it did not work and after landing I asked the ground crew to make it work. The work took a great deal of time but they were unable to fix it. This was time wasted and delayed my departure by over two hours; the radio would not be of any use to me after I flew beyond its range anyway, but I might need it on my return, if I returned. This lost time would make my return very late, possibly after nightfall, and left me with a feeling of foreboding and apprehension as I made the take off. It was late afternoon and still warm as I gained altitude over the North Sea but I felt icy cold inside. I crossed the coast of Holland at 28,000 feet, flying east just north of the Zuider Zee, hoping the German radar stations would not trigger fighter interception. There were no clouds to be seen anywhere at any altitude, the visibility was crystal clear and the ground could also be seen with crystal clarity. I decided to fly to the most distant target first, it being the one farthest away from England, and hoped it might tend to give the Luftwaffe a false impression as to what my course and intentions might be. This was a pre-damage operation and the Central Interpretation Unit at Medmenham, in addition to other things, would compare the photographs I took to photographs taken the day after the targets had been bombed and assess the damage caused by the attacks. It also provided a first-hand report of the weather for the impending bomber attacks, except that I had no radio to give it. It was necessary to cover many targets on a pre-damage operation to prevent the enemy from knowing which targets might be subjected to attack; this did not give me a happy feeling knowing that the Luftwaffe was fresh during this sortie and that the number of targets to be covered would prolong my exposure to interception. It was also an irritating thought that the glory boys, the pilots who took the post-damage assessment photographs, only had to cover the targets that had been bombed that night with the Luftwaffe possibly tired and on the ground after the night's operations. Also annoying was the fact that the post-bombing-raid photographs were the ones used for publication in the newspapers. But these thoughts I dismissed from my mind; the only thoughts that I could entertain as I flew across northern Germany was how to reach and effectively cover the targets and hope that I would be able to return with the information.

Reaching Stettin, I made the first photographic runs over the town before proceeding north to photograph the Heinkel factory and the airfield located on the west side of the estuary that emptied into the Baltic (see plate 10). This was where bombers that were attacking Britain were built. Sitting in my unarmed aircraft at 28,000 feet in crystal-clear weather it would be an understatement to say that I was unconcerned about my vulnerability but, although I felt icy cold, I was ready to deal with any situation that might arise, hopefully in a calm calculated way. Despite the time spent over the targets of Stettin and the Heinkel works, I left breathing a sigh of relief that neither anti-aircraft fire nor Luftwaffe fighters had attacked me and my tension eased slightly as I altered course toward my next target.

Flying five miles high over eastern Germany, hundreds of miles from any safety, the feeling of utter loneliness was of such intensity that no words could describe it. However, there was relief knowing that the rest of the targets were in the direction of home; even the inward icy cold I felt after take off felt a degree or two warmer. But the gauntlet of hundreds of miles still had to be run to reach safety and a friendly face, and the time it would take to cover the targets on the way back would give the enemy greater opportunity to intercept, but that was something I did not want to think about and I headed toward the next target – Rostock.

Rostock, located a few miles south of the Baltic near Peenemunde, did not require many runs to get full coverage. After Rostock, flying west, I photographed airfields and towns including Warnemunde, Wismar and then flew south-west to Lubeck (see plate 11).

Flying further inland I photographed Wensendorf and skirted the south side of Hamburg to photograph the airfield at Stade. For good measure, I used up surplus film and photographed unscheduled targets such as Cuxhaven at the mouth of the Elbe. With a sigh of relief I then set course for Heligoland.

After leaving each of the targets the icy feeling inside me had melted just a little and, as I flew over the island of Heligoland, I could barely believe my good fortune at not having been intercepted in such crystal-clear weather with no clouds to hide in anywhere and headed west out over the North Sea. I felt so relieved I even started to feel good. Now all I had to do to was to avoid any interception flying past the Frisian Islands. I minimised that possibility by putting the nose down and increasing speed. I had avoided capture, or worse, and wondered whether I had outsmarted the enemy or, as was more likely, been just plain lucky. With the threat of interception diminishing as I sped across the North Sea toward England, realising a new threat was looming and that I did not have any idea of how to cope with it, it was literally a real 'nightmare'. As I reduced altitude it got dark rapidly as I reached lower altitudes, and it was already dark as I crossed back over England. It was not just dark; it was pitch black with no stars or illumination in the British wartime blackout. I could not even tell where the ground was. My Spitfire was not equipped for night flying and had no lights even to illuminate the instrument panel and no radio to seek assistance; I was calm and knew I had to cope with it on my own.

I was supposed to land and refuel at Ludham on my return as I would be almost out of fuel, but this was not possible as it was already dark. Landing at an unfamiliar airfield without lights or radio in the dark was virtually impossible even if I could find one. Not having a radio really hit home; it was not just dark – it was pitch black and the impossibility of being able to find an airfield was scary enough. As I was almost out of fuel, I would have to make a blind landing or bale out when the engine stopped; there were no other choices. I could only hope I was able to find an airfield. Benson seemed to be the only possibility but, in pitch darkness, even if I don't run out of fuel first, how? I felt as alone as I had over Stettin, but with no help I had to find a way out of this mess. All I could do was hope that I was flying in the right direction. I was feeling angry with myself for not having ignored the faulty radio that had made my return so late when a momentary glimmer of light on what may have been a hillside gave me a moment of hope. I guessed it to be Wendover in the Chiltern Hills.

The guess was apparently right. Although I do not know how, I felt I might have found Benson and made an approach on to what I hoped might be a runway, but the runways at Benson were blacktops and it was impossible to be sure in the blackness that it really was a runway. Now was the critical moment and I throttled back, holding off for touchdown, not knowing how high I was above the ground, keeping my fingers crossed for what I could only hope was a runway and that my height from the ground was not too great to survive the ensuing stall. Incredibly it was a runway but, in the pitch black of night and with no means of being able to judge my height above the ground, the aeroplane just quit flying and found its own way down with such a resounding jolt that I thought the undercarriage would come up through the wings. They didn't and the Spitfire rolled to a stop. Although the landing did not appear to have done any damage to the aircraft, it did something that the technicians had been unable to accomplish at Ludham – it jolted the radio back to life, but what use was that to me now? Taxiing the aircraft was impossible. I shut the engine down and just left it where it was. In my concentration on finding an airfield I had not dared to give the slightest thought of how much petrol I might have left; it was probably better that I did not know.

There was nothing to suggest that they had expected me to return. I remembered my first night flight at SFTS when I could not imagine on a dark night in the blackout how lost you would be without the flare path or what you would do. I had just found out, without even any cockpit lights. I still don't know how I did it. No response to my arrival appeared to be happening, just total silence. Having spent more than seven hours in the air, in addition to the wasted time on the ground at Ludham, I was tired; it had been a long day.

With the feeling of being abandoned, I had to find my way to where someone might recognise that I still existed. It would be a long walk to the other side of the airfield in the pitch-black night and not easy. After stumbling along the perimeter for some distance, a security vehicle patrolling the airfield loomed out of the darkness and gave me a ride back to 'civilisation'. I was unable to tell them where my aeroplane was parked; I did not know. I had found my way to the far reaches of Germany and back in impossible circumstances and the least they could do was to find the aeroplane and unload the camera magazines without my help. It was their problem and I no longer cared. Flying that aeroplane back in the pitch blackness of night and successfully finding and landing back at my base was impossible, but I had done it. I had made my day's contribution to the war effort.

At the debriefing they seemed surprised that I had covered every target. An officer who had previously covered just the targets of Stettin and Rostock was awarded the Distinguished Flying Cross; later I was chewed out for not reporting that I had also covered Cuxhaven, but I was only a sergeant. After being given the usual tin of fruit juice, although hungry I forwent the operational meal and, filled with disgust, went straight to my room, got into bed and fell asleep immediately. I had had enough for one day.

The following morning I had no need to rush as I had been relieved of duty for the day. I missed breakfast and went into Wallingford and had lunch at a restaurant. I spent the afternoon relaxing in a pretty area where the bridge crossed over the river Thames. There I tried to sort out the confused thoughts that had been running through my head. At my age I had not formed much of an image of myself, but constant criticism did not contribute to my having a good self-image, but flying this operation, which I had considered a suicide mission when I took off from Ludham with the firm belief that I would not return, made me think that, whatever else might be said about me, I was sure of one thing: regardless of what other people might think about my character or lack of it – I was not a coward. But no one had said 'Well done' or 'Glad you made it back'. I felt recognition was something they gave only to other people and I was nothing more than expendable.

The losses that 543 Squadron had experienced the previous year had tempered my feelings of vulnerability, but the success of this sortie, recognised or not, fortified me, knowing it was something that, despite the difficulties, I could repeat if ordered, although I'm not too sure that I could repeat the blind-flying return in the dark (see plate 12).

A few days later I went on leave and, together with Flight Sergeant Flanagan, I flew a Miles Master to a small grass airfield at Braunstone on the outskirts of Leicester. While Flight Sergeant Flanagan flew the aircraft back to Benson, I walked from the airfield across the road to the Everard's pub, appropriately named 'The Airmen's Rest'. There was no bus service into Leicester and, it being a long walk, I hoped I might be able to obtain a ride to the tram terminal at Western Park. I was soon offered a lift into Leicester where I caught the corporation bus from Humberstone Gate to Catherine Street. After getting off at the Coronation pub stop, I walked the short distance home with a heightened awareness of how wonderful it was to experience the English spring.

Chapter 8

An African Holiday

I hoped my dedication to duty and performance had made me an asset and cemented my place as an operational pilot at Benson. After two days of being on leave a police officer knocked on the door and informed me that I had to return to Benson immediately. The most expedient way of returning was to drive my recently purchased 1932 Rover Pilot back to Benson; the return was interrupted by a connecting rod coming through the side of the engine and to arrive back at the station on time there was no choice but to abandon the car on the grass verge until I could do something about it and hitchhike the rest of the way to Benson. Wondering why it was so urgent that I should be recalled from routine leave after only two days, I was ordered to fly acceptance tests on two Mk XI Spitfires. The first I flew was EN407 (the aircraft's registration number); it performed satisfactorily and the fuel consumption was only 32 gallons per hour, less than the acceptable consumption rate of 36 gallons per hour and I was impressed with its overall qualities. When I had the engine cowlings removed I found that there was no oil residue on the engine which was unusual because it was rare for an engine not to leak a small amount of oil.

I was told that an officer's first consideration is the welfare of his men or have I got it the wrong way round?

The following day I flight-tested the second Spitfire (see plate 13), still wondering what the rush was all about as there were plenty of other pilots who could have accomplished the tests instead of me. The 'hurry up and wait' routine being imposed on me had resulted in unnecessary damage to the engine of my car. The following morning, 2 May 1943, I was ordered to fly EN407 to RAF Station Portreath in Cornwall en route to Africa that day – just like that; no embarkation leave, no consideration of my not wanting to go overseas. I guess I was for some reason not wanted at Benson and, due to having absolutely no notice of this dramatic change, I was never able to recover my car which the authorities impounded and imposed a fine for my 'abandoning' it. Of course, there was no way to recover the cost of the loss and I realised I was not considered deserving of any consideration. At Portreath I met Flying Officer Cline who informed me that I would accompany him on a formation flight to Gibraltar and then continue on to Maison Blanche airfield near Algiers. This confused me. Did they not think I could find my way on my own and needed to be guided by the officer or was it perhaps the other way round? Apparently, without any advanced notice, I was being deported to No. 682 PR Squadron, based at Maison Blanche, Algeria. The briefing and navigation information having been made and the aircraft readied for flight, the time for departure arrived. Take off was uneventful and, as instructed, I formated on the starboard wing of Flying Officer Cline's Spitfire. We climbed to 28,000 feet on a southerly course across the Bay of Biscay; the course was to cross into Spain over the north-western city of La Coruña. We made the landfall at La Coruña, changed course and flew due south as ordered to fly along the border separating Spain from Portugal, despite it being against international law to fly in the airspace of neutral countries; but this was war. Shortly after crossing into Spain, the engine of Cline's Spitfire lost power. In the past I had experienced the type of problem that he was experiencing and gave him advice over the radio, the VHF proving useful, on how to clear the vapour lock in his fuel system that I knew it to be; unfortunately it did not seem that the officer felt that the advice of a non-commissioned officer could be of help and we steadily lost height. After losing thousands of feet with his engine only running spasmodically and his compounding the problem by not following the instructions that I knew from past experience would solve his problem, I felt I could not abandon him. It was my duty to remain with him and do my best to try and help resolve his problem. In formation, knowing that, in the denser atmosphere of the lower altitudes, our range was being reduced and the amount of fuel that we were carrying might not be sufficient for us to reach Gibraltar, I kept repeating on the radio the correct way to clear the vapour lock. We were down to 2,000 feet before he listened and his engine started to run smoothly again. Having spent so much time at low altitude crossing the Iberian peninsula at low altitude, the anticipated time of the flight had almost doubled. Our remaining supply of petrol was now very low, so low that when we arrived over Cadiz our fuel gauges were on empty. Although I was very worried, all I could do was hope we had enough petrol left to get to the Rock of Gibraltar and land. At an altitude of only 1,000 feet, with our fuel gauges hard on empty, Flying Officer Cline turned on to a straight-line course to Gibraltar, it being the shortest distance to the runway. I watched him enter the cloud covering Europa Point and, knowing that Europa Point reached an elevation of over 3,000 feet, I was afraid he would kill himself and shouted over the radio 'Come out of that cloud, it has a rock lining, I will put you onto the runway.' Fortunately, Cline, who had ignored all my previous advice, but now appeared to be panicking, followed my instructions and came out of the cloud. I told him to formate on my port side and led him around Europa Point. Foregoing the required identification procedures, we approached Gibraltar from the south and I lined him up to land westbound on the runway that protruded out into the Bay of Algeciras. As I guided Flying Officer Cline's aircraft down to the threshold of the runway and could see that he would land safely, I opened my throttle and with my fingers crossed made a turn to the left to circle the Rock before I could land my own aircraft. With my petrol gauges having been hard on empty since Cadiz, I was expecting the engine to cut at any moment. The gods must have smiled on me as I rounded the Rock and made an uneventful landing. At last I was able to breath a sigh of relief after all that strain. Having been to Gibraltar before, I taxied to the correct parking spot and shut the engine down.

But where did Flying Officer Cline park his aircraft? I could not see it anywhere but knew it had to be around somewhere; I was anxious to hear any comments about the flight and hopefully he would tell me that he had appreciated the help I had provided on the very stressful flight. Secretly, though, I would really have liked to have chewed him out for putting us into such danger by not listening to my instructions on how to clear the fuel-vapour lock. But I could not help wondering if he realised that if he had not followed my instructions to come out of the cloud covering Europa Point he would have been killed. I was happy that I had been able to guide him to a safe landing and it made me feel good that I had done the right thing throughout the flight from England, even if it had proved precarious. However, by not listening to me, he had jeopardised my life, and it would have been a court martial offence for me to tell him what a stupid jerk he was.

I eventually located Flying Officer Cline, but not his aeroplane; his flaps had blown up as he touched down due to the rubber seal of the flap selector switch rupturing, a known shortcoming of the Spitfire's flap system, but he had failed to immediately return the switch to the 'up' position to retain enough pneumatic pressure to operate the brakes. So, not having any pneumatic pressure, he had no brakes and stopped his aircraft by retracting the undercarriage. The aircraft had slid to the side of the runway and skidded to a stop between aircraft being assembled there. He was lucky that he did not hit any of the aircraft or the personnel who were assembling them. I thought to myself *I know that I have made mistakes but why do I seem have better judgement as a pilot than Flying Officer Cline and have to address such stupid idiots as 'Sir'?* I could only wonder how I had managed to find myself in the midst of pilots who were so inept, and officers at that – and they were my superiors?

It would have been bad enough if that were the end of the story, but insult was added to injury. The next morning, I went to the runway to have my aircraft made ready for the last leg of the flight to Algiers but, not being an officer, I had to walk all the way to the runway. This took much longer than Flying Officer Cline who was provided with transport. Arriving at the dispersal my aircraft was missing. I found it incredible when I was told that the officer had taken my aeroplane, together with my belongings, without even telling me or providing me with any alternatives on how to get to Algiers. Surely the officer could not have disdained such lower peons as non-commissioned personnel so much that he would have abandoned one without a word even after in effect he had saved his life. Feeling as if I had been demoted from superboy to trashboy, I wondered why was a non-commissioned pilot considered to be worthless. I would have been even angrier if I had known that I was also an officer: although I did not know it, I had been commissioned on 13 February 1943, but no one had bothered to tell me.

Cline had not expressed the slightest appreciation for saving his life the day before and had now abandoned me, perhaps to make it appear that I had flown the other aircraft and crashed it. Why else would he have left me there unable to defend myself about anything he might say, or was it the other way round and he was afraid that if I had the first word it might reflect badly on his sub-standard performance since leaving England? I was probably exaggerating things in my own mind, but what else could have been the reason? I had done nothing to deserve being left in such a compromising situation. Now, having been apparently dismissed as unworthy of consideration, this was not as I had been told: that an officer's first consideration was 'the welfare of his men'. It left me in a very difficult position. I did not have an aeroplane, I did not have any credentials or orders, and there was no one of authority to whom I could turn or who would understand my position, or for that matter would even believe such an unlikely story.

I was so angry that I wondered if I should just have let him run into the mountain at Point Europa or even bothered to try to help solve his fuel problem over Spain and left him to his own devices. Not believing me, as I had learned in the past, was the most likely outcome. After all, if a sergeant came up with a story like that, and with no papers or being able to show how he had even arrived at Gibraltar, who would believe him? The result would most likely be that I would be put in detention until the matter could be sorted out and that could be at the end of the war; but, then, that might not be such a bad idea. Right now I wondered why I was risking my life in such a morass of stupidity and being looked down upon when it appeared that I was a hell of a lot more proficient as a pilot than the officers I was supposed to look up to. I was so angry with this that I decided that I was going to find some way out of this and face Flying Officer Cline down, even if it meant a court martial. I felt demeaned and humiliated at being treated in such an off-hand manner. Had I not, even though without risk to myself, saved the officer's life? Although, come to think of it, by doing what I thought was the right thing I had placed myself at considerable risk too, flying with only fumes of petrol left. By now I realised that I had unerringly committed myself to fighting the war, but did I have to do it in the company of such arrogantly stupid people? I was beginning to think that people like that were more of a threat to the war effort than I had once considered myself to be. Although in my experience I had observed a number of officers to whom I looked up, now there were many I looked down on; and I was only a sergeant.

At Benson I had watched an officer enter the circuit and, after lowering his undercarriage to land, put his flaps down and I saw that he had the same problem that I had had at Squires Gate – only one flap came down. The pilot retracted the flap and his undercarriage and went around the circuit. After collecting his thoughts, he made the decision to land without flaps. However, he did forget something – the undercarriage; it was only when the propeller started cutting ridges in the runway that he realised his shortcoming and opened his throttle to go around but with his damaged propeller he was unable to keep his aircraft in the air. He made it as far as a farmer's field on the far side of the airfield perimeter where it slid to a standstill in the soft forgiving earth. I was the first person to reach the scene and, although there was little damage to the aircraft and the pilot was uninjured, when I asked why he did not put his undercarriage down, Flying Officer Irons said that he did. I pointed out that the undercarriage selector was still in the 'up' position and, to help the officer save face, I put it into the 'down' position.

Now I thought that if I had been flying the aeroplane I would probably be facing a charge or ordered to sweep the officers' mess, not because of the 'accident' but because I was a member of the lower class. No, of course I don't have a chip on my shoulder: why should I?

But now I was stuck in Gibraltar without papers, no aeroplane, and no orders. I was supposed to be at Maison Blanche, but how was I supposed to get there – swim? How could I possibly have gotten into a mess like this? But, more importantly, how could I get out of it, realising that if I was at 682 Squadron in Maison Blanche I would not be 'absent without official leave' because that was where I was supposed to be. But I was not at Maison Blanche; I was in Gibraltar without an aeroplane, or orders, or any means of getting to Algiers. I wondered if I could find a way to get there. It might get me out of trouble, but I knew I would be judged by what was said about me, not the facts of what had actually happened. At this point if I had been in England I would have said to hell with the war and deserted. I had run out of patience with the lack of consideration and the abuse. I was tired of being on the bottom rung of the ladder and stepped on. Why was I risking my life for a system that failed to recognise that all pilots are equal? My sense of humour had not only been reduced, it had disappeared in a cloud of smoke. I wondered if the Luftwaffe treated their pilots like this? No! They probably shot people like me, so I had better just grin and bear it. There is no need to laugh; things will pick up in the next act after the interval, said he hopefully.

Although I had been on the Rock of Gibraltar before, I had no idea of what the movements of aircraft might be in the Mediterranean theatre. Among the numerous aircraft scattered around the airfield I hoped I might be able to find one whose destination was Maison Blanche and thumb a ride and started walking. First, I considered the bombers, but they were mostly American bombers of the USAAF. I did not approach them thinking that they might be suspicious of me. After a lot of walking I stumbled on an RAF Douglas C-47 Dakota with a two-man crew about to board. I expected that their destination would be some place other than Algiers, but I asked anyway and found they were actually going to Maison Blanche. I told them my story and was surprised that they believed me and invited me on board. Although I did not obtain the names of the two officer pilots, I wished that there were more like them in the RAF.

Having managed to arrive at Maison Blanche, not a word was mentioned about the previous day and my delay in arriving there, nor did anyone ask how I had resolved the dilemma of being abandoned in Gibraltar even though I had reported to my squadron in a war zone without papers, travel documents, etc., etc., etc. I don't think they cared whether I arrived or not but, being there, I was told that I was now a member of No. 682 PR Squadron. Someone might have at least said welcome. I was informed that we were now a part of the United States Army Air Forces' (USAAF) North West Africa Photographic Reconnaissance Wing (NAPRW). I was now with the United States Army Air Forces under the command of General Karl Spaatz. I would be flying in an American-commanded element of the Mediterranean Allied Air Forces with No. 682 Squadron under command of Lieutenant Colonel Elliot Roosevelt. I suppose I now had to replace my upper-class English accident with an American drawl when addressing my new commanding officer and how do you address the son of the President of the United States, Franklin D. Roosevelt? This war was becoming a tad demanding.

However, I was to find that, as a pseudo-American, I would be shown more consideration by the United States forces than I was ever shown by the British forces. After one flight to familiarise myself with the surrounding area, I was sent on my first operational sortie, to Sardinia. The operation was successful, except for a minor problem – the cameras didn't work. Equipment failure almost certainly blamed on Gremlins was to plague the squadron for all the summer months. Equipment failure could be coped with, but when the equipment was the aircraft itself it was a larger problem, a problem I was fated to try to solve more than once in the not too distant future. I felt some foreboding about being press-ganged into becoming a member of this squadron when I was informed that one of the 682 Squadron pilots had been killed on the day of my arrival. I surmised that he must have been killed in the vicinity of the airfield, since a funeral had already been held at the local burial ground. I did not want to find out how he had been killed.

There were very few service people wearing uniforms other than those of the United States' forces. Their relaxed attitude to discipline was a pleasant and welcome change from the rigid, uncaring, disciplinarian attitude of the RAF. My only contact previously with members of the United States Army Air Forces had taken place a few weeks before with a few American pilots at Benson. The American pilots flew Lockheed F-4 Lightning photographic-reconnaissance aircraft from the airfield at Mount Farm that was now occupied by the USAAF. They had gathered in my room in the sergeants' quarters at Benson and plied Jackie Dearden and I with questions about how to go about flying operational missions over enemy territory. Neither Jack nor I felt that we were qualified to give much advice because we had so little experience ourselves, but we had been impressed by these American officers in their impeccable uniforms who did not fit the boastful image that had typified the Americans as being know-alls who could drop a bomb from 30,000 feet into a pickle barrel.

These officers were rather humble and were really looking for any first-hand information that might better prepare them to fly missions over enemy territory. Obviously, they were smart enough to seek first-hand information rather than trust the theoretical brainwashing that they had been subjected to during training. Jack and I gave them what information we thought might be of any help and were shocked when told to stop addressing them as 'Sir'; they said 'We should be addressing you as "Sir", you have flown operational missions and we have not flown any.' Being given respect for what we had done rather than being addressed only by our non-commissioned rank of sergeant was something that we had not now and would not experience in the RAF in the future; we figured that the informal Americans can't be all bad.

The pilots of 682 Squadron were accommodated in a requisitioned mansion. Although not luxurious, it was satisfactory, but I was finding the heat of North Africa to be oppressive in contrast to the cool temperatures of England. The unit had an office on the airfield that was entirely American; there was a flight crewroom made from a large converted crate in which a section of an aircraft fuselage had been shipped from the United States. A communal mess had been constructed by the USAAF on the airfield and the food was good, the 'menu' including many items from the USA that I had either forgotten existed or were items that I had not previously heard of, such as tinned Vienna sausages among the many other canned items. Ice-cold lemonade, made from lemon powder, was always available; however, there was a lack of fresh foods and it was mostly just tinned food. But it was available twenty-four hours a day and anyone could use it any time he felt hungry or thirsty. The communal mess had but one drawback; there was no place to sit, necessitating eating standing up. It was quite different to anything I had experienced in the RAF. There appeared to be no privilege in rank in the communal mess; all ranks, both commissioned and non-commissioned, ate in the same way, with no discrimination. The Americans may have been inexperienced when they entered the war, but they appeared very experienced when it came to the way their service personnel were treated in the field. What to me were luxury items were readily available; they included gramophones with records of radio shows, UFO shows with well-known movie stars, music records, playing cards, etc., even many flavours of ice cream. It seemed the first thing that the American forces did when they moved into a new town was to set-up an ice cream manufacturing facility. Their K-rations contained snacks and even three or four cigarettes and were available to anyone who wanted them, but the only alcohol available was Bier Stella, a local lager-style beer, and local wine, but no liquor.

The long solitary runway on the airfield was in constant use, mostly by American aircraft ranging from fighters to heavy bombers, together with transports landing and taking off continuously. The atmosphere was one of being all-American with the exception of a few rarely seen uniforms of other countries. Uniforms worn in the Mediterranean theatre were tropical, but the US forces did not have an issue of shorts, as did the British forces, and their uniforms tended to be rather informal in the field. I felt comfortable in the company of the United States forces. They seemed competent yet unassuming and they seemed to have a trait that I thought was effective: they were experts in the art of what they called 'moonlight-requisitioning', finding a means of obtaining whatever was needed urgently without the delay and red tape of going through channels. I felt less restricted than I had felt in Great Britain, although I felt resentment at being posted to North Africa after having gained an understanding and, hopefully, created a good impression by the number of difficult operations I had flown from England. I had become comfortable with the dangers there and was willing to continue flying operations there until the end of the war, if I survived. The missions conducted by the North-west African Photographic Reconnaissance Wing (NAPRW) were flown by both the USAAF, flying their F-4 Lightnings, and 682 Squadron, flying their Spitfires. Operations were conducted covering targets in the western Mediterranean and southern Europe from the Maison Blanche airfield a few miles east of Algiers.

As part of the MAAF, there was a difference from the RAF; no pre- or post-operational intelligence briefings were held; we were just told what targets to cover. Difficulties and dangers encountered on the operations went unrecorded, except for the informal notes that we made in our pilots' logbooks.

The ground forces campaign that had started with the invasion of North-West Africa, Operation TORCH, had advanced to a point 100 miles or so east of Algiers. Maison Blanche, from which we operated, was a few miles from Algiers and required long flights across the Mediterranean to reach targets ranging from Sicily in the south of Italy and north to the border of Switzerland and targets in the south of France, together with Mediterranean islands and targets in North Africa. Although considerable progress had been made in the effort to join up with the British forces that had advanced from El Alamein almost to Tunisia, the German forces were still not beaten in Africa as evidenced by the battle of the Kasserine Pass and the huge tank battle to the west of Tunisia on the plain of La Sabalqa.

I flew operations covering many targets including Sardinia, Corsica, being suitable for the south of France and Italy, reaching the targets on the long flights over the Mediterranean in some aircraft that belonged more in a scrapyard rather than flying long distances across the Mediterranean. Such questionable aircraft failed to provide any feeling of security. Over northern Europe, I had been used to short overwater flights and facing the enemy for long periods; here I was flying long overwater flights for short exposure to the enemy; and when flying doubtful aircraft with only one engine it was hazardous. The long flights over the water left me with nothing to occupy my mind but my thoughts: I considered the circumstances of my becoming a pilot and wondered if I had made the right decision by avoiding conscription into the Army. Only a few soldiers would actually see combat and come face to face with the enemy; the vast majority would serve in supporting roles, but they were all necessary for the furtherance of the war effort. However, such thoughts were redundant, and I felt a degree of satisfaction when facing the enemy although there was little appreciation shown. But somehow I felt that I had been backed into a corner in North Africa. It had seemed inappropriate to send me there, taking away the satisfaction I felt flying the more dangerous skies of northern Europe. I was left with the feeling of hopelessness that I had run out of elbow room and would just have to put up with these long overwater flights and do my job. But there was one saving grace, I enjoyed flying.

Although I had little trepidation about the long flights over water a few of the targets required only short overwater flights, such as operations to cover airfields and ports in Sardinia, ranging from Cagliari in the south to airfields such as Vila Cedro in the north. The territory appeared markedly different to the targets in northern Europe, probably due to there being very few clouds. But, even when aircraft performed properly, some sorties were flown with nothing to show for the effort when non-functioning cameras rendered the operation a useless exercise, endemic in this theatre. It was frustrating, after the risks involved in flying the mission, to be told that the cameras had failed and that the risk had been for nothing. It was frustrating that it was something you could not be aware of or do anything about, but I felt it was a blemish on my previously perfect operational record in operations over northern Europe. Risking my life 'paying for territory' with no payback was frustrating. Were the insidious Gremlins catching up with us? Starting to gain height on another flight across the Mediterranean to cover targets in the south of France the Gremlins started cycling the propeller RPM up and down, making it appear dangerous to continue the long flight across the Mediterranean. I felt it better to be safe rather than sorry and returned to Maison Blanche where the reaction made me feel that I should just have continued; it did not enhance my reputation. Faulty aeroplanes and equipment created an uneasy feeling about crossing hundreds of miles of the Mediterranean to reach targets, especially when the sortie did not provide results.

I flew a Spitfire Mk IX fighter equipped with two 20mm cannon after days filled with frustration. The aeroplane was borrowed from a fighter squadron and in excellent condition. I practised firing the cannon at a rock in the Mediterranean, and was disappointed when I pressed the firing button on the control column, thinking the guns had malfunctioned. The disappointment disappeared when I heard a noise like galloping horses and felt the aeroplane shaking. I thought I had missed the target until I saw flashes on the rock as the shells struck home. After returning to the airfield and landing, the thought crossed my mind that I might have been a good fighter pilot under different circumstances, but the rock was not shooting back at me as I had experienced flying over enemy-held territory in northern Europe.

From the cool, and often cold, rainy weather of Britain to the warm sunshine of the southern Mediterranean would be a welcome change for most personnel but I found it too hot and felt physically tired without the energy that I normally enjoyed. This, together with a loss of appetite, and not feeling my normal self, I put down to the change of climate. The next few weeks were occupied flying operations with targets ranging from Sardinia and Corsica to southern France and Italy. The news that the French fleet had been scuttled in November 1942, as ordered by the French Admiral Darlan, who had then been assassinated on Christmas Eve, had been a welcome relief since the potential threat of the French naval units to the Allies in the Mediterranean was therefore neutralised.

France had been under the control of the Vichy government and was now occupied by the Germans who controlled much of Scandinavia and all of Europe from their front in Russia to the Spanish border. The only bright spot that the western Allies had was that the German and Italian forces were suffering reversals in Africa.

Not being paid and having no money invites a little larceny?
Well not exactly!

Despite all the epoch-making news, when not flying I hung around the airfield at Maison Blanche twiddling my thumbs wondering what the little yellow packets were on the floor of the flight hut that were being swept up and discarded as rubbish. Being curious, I pulled open the flap of one of them to find what was in them. It contained a handkerchief-size silk map of Italy and France, together with twenty-six silver certificate US dollars with a red seal; there were also four French 20-franc coins. Although the dollars had little or no practical use in North Africa, there being little or nothing worth purchasing anyway, I surmised that the maps could be easily concealed and presumed the purpose was to help find your way and evade capture if shot down over enemy territory. These packets were discarded by the USAAF aircrews, to whom they appeared to have little or no value. Although $26 seemed to be a large amount of money to me, the dollars were no use in Algiers as only Algerian francs were valid as currency. Even so, the disdain that the Americans appeared to have for the money made me envious. After all I received under 10 shillings a day, which was less than two dollars, and that was before tax. But, in any case, it was all conjecture since no one appeared to draw any pay in that theatre as there was practically nothing to buy anyway. But why would the US dollars be included in what turned out to be 'Escape packets'? I was told that American dollars were valued by the people of France who would be happy to receive them as a gesture when they aided downed airmen to evade capture by the Germans and be repatriated. Repatriation was accomplished by French freedom fighters who helped Allied airmen to escape from enemy territory, often by negotiating the passes through the Pyrenees and on through Spain to Portugal. To me the American dollars seemed a very small gesture to make, considering that the penalty for aiding Allied airmen was death. But this still left the 20-franc coins unexplained. Twenty francs was virtually nothing, so why include them? Then the penny dropped. The weight of each coin seemed heavy and I realised that these 20-franc 'Louis' coins were made of solid gold. At last there arose a circumstance to arouse my spirit of entrepreneurship. I knew that there had to be a use for them and, since they were being discarded and swept away as rubbish, what use could they be put to? Having observed that many people had gold teeth, surely dentists would now have difficulty obtaining gold. After a little investigation in Algiers, I struck gold or, more literally, Algerian francs. I had four and sold each of them for 4,500 Algerian francs. Although the 1,000-franc notes (about the size of a Scottish £5 note) were legal tender, they really had little real value as there was nothing to buy. I just enjoyed revelling in not being penniless or, to be more precise, franc-less.

Flight training by the USAAF

Lieutnant Colonel Drue of the USAAF called me into the office near the entrance to Maison Blanche airfield and gave me cause to remember when I had walked around the airfield in Gibraltar looking at the many aircraft dispersed in different areas both on and around the base. There were many British-built aircraft and, in addition, a large number of aircraft manufactured in the USA, including RAF Hudson bombers, there. I had been impressed by an American P-38 with its twin fuselage and two Allison engines. I had been told that the propellers rotated in opposite directions and recalled that this was the type of aircraft that the American flyers at Mount Farm were equipped with. The P-38 appeared to be too big to be flown without first being checked out by an instructor, but none had been built with dual controls; I wondered how pilots were converted to fly them.

Lieutenant Colonel Dunn showed me how when he converted me to P-38s by telling me to go over to the flight line and fly one – so much for dual instruction. After pulling down the mounting step, located in the rear of the nacelle containing the pilot's compartment, of an F-4, the photographic-reconnaissance version of the P-38, and climbing into the cockpit, the colonel provided rudimentary instructions on how to turn on the inverters and streamline the radiators and oil coolers after take off, warning me to ensure that the canopy sides were closed before take off. The only other instructions were to use 45 inches of mercury for take off, put the landing gear down at 160 mph, start the approach at 1,000 feet two miles from the threshold, deploy full flaps and carry 15 inches of mercury with an approach speed over the threshold of 90 mph.

The colonel helped me start the engines and then left me to my own devices. Being a so-called qualified pilot, I felt that, at least, I should try and taxi the aeroplane to a spot where I was not observable and try to remember the instructions he had given me. I found the aircraft easy enough to taxi, although using the toe brakes, which were entirely different to the brakes used on British aircraft, took a little getting used to. I managed to taxi it to a spot at the east end of the runway close to the take-off point but hidden behind other aircraft. I then tried to translate what I had been told, and could remember, into terms that made sense. First I figured that the amount of power indicated in RAF aircraft as 'boost pressure' where zero boost was the equivalent of atmospheric pressure would be indicated as 32 inches on the power indicators of this aircraft. I then checked the instruments I would need. The basic blind-flying panel, containing such instruments as the airspeed indicator, altitude indicator, artificial horizon, rate of climb and descent etc., was pretty much the same as the ones that I was used to in RAF machines, so I concentrated on locating the landing-gear indicator, the flap indicator, the switches to control the radiator and oil-cooler flaps, trim tab and generally familiarising myself with the cockpit layout and the control locations. The use of the inverters escaped me, but they were switched on and I knew that was correct. Taxiing having proved easy enough, the feeling of being lost eased a little as I taxied to the threshold of the runway for take off. The tricycle landing gear provided an unrestricted forward view, different to a single-engine fighter with the nose obstructing you from seeing forward; I could see the entire runway in front of me. This did install a little more confidence, but I had never flown an aircraft with tricycle landing gear before and had no idea how to handle it, but I expected I was about to find out. With the F-4 pointed straight down the centre of the runway, I opened the throttles to 45 inches of mercury and the aeroplane accelerated smoothly down the runway. It was easy to keep straight as there was no torque due to the propellers spinning in opposite directions and, as the aircraft lifted off the ground, it seemed easy to fly and I felt at home in it immediately.

After retracting the landing gear, I climbed to the pattern altitude of 1,000 feet, adjusted the power and RPM settings and trimmed the aircraft for level flight. As I streamlined the radiator and oil-cooler flaps, I wondered why I had thought it would require a great deal of skill to fly it. On the downwind leg, with Algiers ahead, I slowed the aircraft to the correct speed for extension of the landing gear and selected the landing-gear lever to the 'down' position until it felt that it had reached its full limit, but I did not feel the drag from the gear being extended, nor did it show to be down on the Selsyn indicator. There was no reflection of the main gear in the polished engine nacelles, so I knew the gear was not down, but decided to make a dummy approach and ask for confirmation of the landing-gear status on the radio. The approach I found was simplicity itself: as I approached the runway I tried to make the radio call but failed. Sure that the landing gear was retracted, I opened the throttles and went around, but first I wanted to see if a red flare would be fired – it was. My not getting the landing gear extended had provided the opportunity for me to fly the aircraft longer and enabled me to practise a go-around procedure and make me more familiar with the type. I also learned that to use the radio it helped to press the button on the left-hand side of the control column wheel. Well, what do you expect when you have not flown an aircraft that was so different to anything that you had flown before? This time on the downwind leg I leaned really hard on the landing-gear selector lever, and to my relief it clicked down, the landing gear extended and the actual touchdown was easy. All I did was level out over the runway and slowly close the throttles and with the tricycle landing gear I hardly felt the wheels touch the runway. After taxiing back to the flight line and shutting down the engines I decided that this aircraft could be flown by little old ladies from Pasadena who only drove their cars to church on Sundays.

However, I expected to be subjected to a chewing-out over my performance when I returned to the crewroom, but this was the United States Army Air Forces and no one made any comment at all. Apparently flying a strange aircraft for the first time in the USAAF was just a matter of course but if it had been the RAF I would have received a tongue lashing. I felt elated that I had flown an aircraft that had seemed such a challenge and flying it had proved to be so easy. I felt good that the USAAF was so easy to get along with. It appeared that the function of supply and demand came into play in the approach of the different services when it came to aircraft operations: the RAF implied 'We want the aeroplane back, it is more important than the pilot', but Lieutenant Colonel Drue's remark was, 'We don't give a hoot about getting the aeroplane back, we want the pilot back, we can always give him another aircraft.' Although the statements basically said the same thing, Colonel Drue's comment implied the comforting feeling that to Americans the pilot was more important than the aeroplane. As I was the only RAF pilot to be checked out on a P-38 (see plate 14), could it have been that they were considering transferring me to fly F-4s instead of Spitfires. It would have been comforting having two engines on those long overwater flights and being enrolled in the USAAF where I seemed to be appreciated could not be all bad.

Taking chances with an aeroplane would not be tolerated by the RAF. When I observed a P-39 Airacobra tumble end over end over Algiers, I thought the pilot would be killed, but I found afterwards that he was an American pilot by the name of Bob Hoover. He had done it deliberately and, although I would have thought it was impossible to recover from the manoeuvre, apparently Bob Hoover made a practice of showing off this trick. After the war he became a well known test and aerobatics pilot in the United States. In the RAF charges would definitely have been considered.

Told by the USAAF to take an aircraft and climb to 30,000 feet and stay up there for five hours did not make any sense to me, but five hours for what? I asked where I was to go and was told to just fly around until the five hours were up. So what else could I do but take a tour of North Africa, then fly towards Gibraltar and back to Algiers. With time still left, I flew south over the Sahara until the five hours were up. After remaining in the air all those hours I still could not figure out the reason for the flight. It was not until several years later that I read in a book why the high-altitude data was needed. Colonel Elliot Roosevelt wanted the information as part of a package to help evaluate and negotiate the purchase of a new photographic-reconnaissance aircraft being developed by Howard Hughes

The relaxed attitude to discipline when operating as part of the United States Army Air Forces compared to the Royal Air Force was less stressful; their officers seemed to look at all personnel as being just civilians wearing a uniform, which they were, and indeed they were themselves. When talking to each other the word 'Sir' was rarely heard, their first names being used most of the time. The attitude towards each other was one of 'We are here to do a job, forget the discipline and let's get the job done'. I felt a lot more comfortable being called Johnny by the Americans by anyone from a private to my commanding officer, Colonel Roosevelt. Genuine concern for their welfare was not the same as 'An officer's first consideration is the welfare of his men'; it was apparent that they were concerned for the welfare of each other and their high morale was reflected in their happy-go-lucky attitude. It was also apparent in their extra-curricular activities such as movies, entertainment provided by USO shows and holding dances attended by other servicewomen and nurses, activities the British forces did not tend to have in that theatre and, although perhaps inexperienced, they knew they were in the war to win.

Although there were British medical services in North Africa, my deteriorating medical condition either went unnoticed or ignored. Being only 19 years of age, I thought I was immune to medical problems and put down my losing weight and loss of energy to the heat. Eventually I noticed that my urine was turning very dark and that my skin was turning yellow and I had a feeling of utter exhaustion. A medic diagnosed yellow jaundice; after two days still feeling exhausted, I returned to operational flying duties. Just before this episode, while on a swimming break at the beach at Cape Matifou, a P-38 buzzed the sands on one engine. I was amazed when an RAF officer mentioned that they thought that the P-38 pilot was me. After two days back on duty with the jaundice being passed off so lightly I assumed it was nothing to be concerned about, but the high temperatures I was experiencing did not go away.

*Of course, in the RAF we were given the best of
medical attention weren't we?*

My not feeling good came to a head at 28,000 feet on my way to targets in the Naples area. The visibility in which I was flying was surrealistic; it started with the blue Mediterranean below and changed as in a ball of cottonwool, from the blue sea turning though grey to pink and back to the blue of the sky. It had an unreal quality with no horizon and felt like flying in a ball of cottonwool. At some point I must have lost consciousness. It was not like nodding off for a few moments, it must have been instant. I had no memory of prior warning, such as faintness or lightheadedness, or even a feeling of sleepiness. When I came to, it was unlike waking up amongst recognisable or familiar things. I did not know who I was or where I was. I was in a surrealistic vacuum encapsulated inside a surrealistic ball of coloured cottonwool trapped inside a strange capsule. I did not know what I was doing there or how I got there. Only as I started to climb out of the capsule did some sense of reality start to return and I realised the capsule I was trying to climb out of was an aeroplane. Slowly my memory was returning. Fortunately, my aircraft was trimmed correctly and still flying straight and level. The aeroplane was functioning correctly, but I was not. I was somewhere over the Mediterranean and not sure what I was supposed to be doing but, as my memory sharpened back into focus, I remembered that I was on my way to cover targets around the Bay of Naples. With my mind clear again I found my way to the target and successfully photographed the Bay of Naples, completing the operation after failing to see enemy aircraft in my flightpath that I was warned of by radio. I landed back at Maison Blanche but I was haunted by what had happened to me and did not know whether I should say anything about it. It was not lack of oxygen – that was on 100 per cent – and the incident had not been preceded by any sense of feeling faint. Had it been lack of oxygen I would not have recovered consciousness as my aircraft was still flying at the same altitude. Being alone at high altitude and suddenly losing consciousness with no apparent reason was scary, but no interest was shown when I reported what had happened. All I did was ask what could have caused it – it was never answered (yellow jaundice, 'Hepatitis', etc. apparently were not considered?). I carried on fulfilling my normal duties. Although facing the enemy was not a problem, there being no answer to my medical problem, together with aircraft that were not airworthy and equipment that regularly failed all tended to erode my self-confidence.

Sometimes an unfortunate occurrence can
have a timely resolution

About this time the non-commissioned officers of 682 Squadron held a rare party at the brasserie in Algiers. Returning to the airfield in the dark in the back of an RAF lorry, a warrant officer, second-class, accused me of kicking him, although I had not kicked him and would not even have thought of kicking him, or anyone else for that matter. Thinking that the WO was probably drunk and would forget all about it in a few minutes, I was soon proved wrong. He ordered me to report to his office at 11:00am the following morning. Not being at my best, with only the rank of sergeant, I was feeling worn down by the sequence of events. Once again, I was being accused of something that I had no knowledge of or even aware of what had happened.

The next morning at 10:00am I was summoned to the adjutant's office. My depression increased and I wondered what I was going to be accused of this time. Arriving promptly at Flight Lieutenant Johnson's office as ordered, the adjutant asked me if I had brought a cot from England. I wondered what prompted such a silly question: how could I have stowed such an item in a Spitfire, the one that Flying Officer Cline had taken from me at Gibraltar; it was not a cargo plane it was a single-seat Spitfire and what few belongings I had been able to carry onboard certainly could not have included a cot. NCOs generally had little besides what they were wearing and so my answer was 'No, Sir'. The adjutant then told me to move my belongings to the officers' quarters as I was no longer an enlisted man and was now Kenneth B. Johnson, a commissioned officer, number 143663, in the Royal Air Force. I hardly had anything to move to the officers' quarters but had great satisfaction in putting the insignia of my new rank of pilot officer on my 'uniform'. I went to the WO's office at 11:00am as he had ordered the night before and blandly asked 'What did you wish to see me about, Warrant Officer?' Of course, the reply was 'Nothing, Sir.' It was one of those few moments that gave me complete satisfaction.

Although I had attended a suitability interview and even ordered officers' uniforms in Oxford, I still thought it to be a mistake as confirmed by my being posted overseas and becoming part of a United States Army

Air Forces command (but still in the RAF). But I was elated at having been promoted to commissioned rank; now I could take it out on those lowly sergeant pilots (just joking), but I did feel ill at ease; from my being a little boy a hundred years ago I had become a competent pilot able to deal with emergencies calmly and efficiently. Despite the commissioning interview, I had not realistically thought that I would ever actually be considered to be officer material. It seemed to be a level of society in which I did not belong; yet I was to find that in this new environment I would be treated by most in just as friendly a manner as if I had come from a wealthy family and had a university education. Didn't they know I had been just a sergeant pilot a few days ago? But I supposed these rapid changes would eventually be accepted by me, but I was still only 19 and Superman was still not my name.

Having meals in the officers' mess was an improvement; the meals were prepared by two Italian prisoners of war who seemed happy to be out of harm's way and were just looking forward to the war ending so that they could go home. They were very accomplished at creating delicious meals from the British raw rations, together with American tinned foods; our opinion was that they were probably cooks in civilian life. I found that being an officer involved additional duties, among which was one of censoring letters that the enlisted men wrote home. Being only a mature youth, I felt that I was intruding in the private lives of men much older than me, but I recognised that this was necessary to make sure that their location was not revealed to anyone and thus prevent security leaks. In any case only the restricted information seemed to register in my mind anyway. In addition to the captured Italians, the motor pool was run by German PoWs who, with the exception of one named Fritz, appeared to be happy to be out of the war and just wanted to get the war over with so that they could go home. They seemed to be trustworthy and certainly did not behave like the despicable Nazis we had been taught to expect; some spoke English and laughingly sang the Second World War ditty mocking Adolf Hitler, which went as follows:

The Führer says, we are the super race,
Sieg Heil, Sieg Heil right in the Führer's face,
Not to love the Führer is a great disgrace,
Sieg Heil, Sieg Heil, right in the Führer's face.

While the German PoWs got a laugh out of singing this song, the odd one, Fritz, would sit there scowling.

The PoWs were assigned work, which they went about conscientiously without supervision. Sergeant Tetley and I went to the sergeants' quarters in a house close by where two Luftwaffe men stripped to the waist were working in the heat, digging a large square hole several feet deep behind the house. Recognising that the men were working very hard, I felt compassionate enough to give them a break from their work and told them 'Nicht Arbeit' and offered them a cigarette, for which they appeared very grateful. Later, as the PoWs were leaving after completing their work, they walked in step with their uniforms immaculate and, as they passed, they gave me the smartest salute that I was ever to receive. How stupid war seemed to be.

At least one operation was, if you cannot call it enjoyable, at least, gratifying. After covering targets in northern Corsica, I flew from Olbia on the isle of Corsica across the Mare Tirreno (Tyrhennian Sea) to Civitavecchia, the port for Rome. Midway, I noticed a ferry that was not under way and I found the reason why as I approached the target. B-17s of the USAAF were still attacking the docks. I waited until they finished and took photographs showing a ship still smoking.

But the Gremlins were persistent. A relatively short operation was scheduled to cover La Maddalena, a natural harbour on the north-east corner of Sardinia, and I was assigned a terrible old wreck of an aeroplane that had somehow been altered to act as a photographic-reconnaissance machine. It was equipped with a huge belly tank and a camera mounted in a wing but, hard as I tried, I could not get the aircraft to climb above 17,000 feet and that was too low to cover the target adequately. To compensate, I flew twice as many runs over the target in an attempt to cover it completely and, after seeing there were no ships in the area, I returned to base and was chewed out by the RAF and told it would be necessary to have the target covered again (what was I expected to do: get out of the aircraft and push it?) although I had probably obtained complete coverage of the target anyway. But where did they dig this old wreck up from and why was I bawled out for what the aircraft was not capable of? At this point I did not care to be criticised for something over which I had no control and I had done my best. In any case it was only a milk run, but it did add to my depression!

A villa in La Marsa had been taken over as the command headquarters for the Tunisian campaign; it was located near Carthage on the north-east tip of the Bay of Tunis. The Northwest African Photographic Reconnaissance Wing moved its Spitfire operations from Maison Blanche to a tiny airstrip near La Marsa. The 'airfield' was no more than a dirt strip that had been used by the Luftwaffe, operating Messerschmitt Bf 109s, three of which were still close by, lying upside down on a dry salt-lake bed. The strip was very short and narrow, bounded on one end by a citrus grove and on the other by an earthen wall lined with stacked German 'Jerrycans' still containing 100-octane fuel. My first glimpse of the field was from the right-hand seat of our B-17, named the 'Mudhen', that I was co-piloting. The strip did not appear long enough to land on, but the skilled hands of Lieutenant Hoover put it down with room to spare.

Is it fair doing this just for the 'fun' of it?

Although at this point the Axis forces were still fighting in North Africa, Tunis had been captured by the Allies, but Axis forces still held territory to the north; fierce fighting was continuing at Bizerte and to the west around Mateur but this did not interfere with our operations from La Marsa which included early morning flights to La Spezia to determine what elements of the Italian Navy, including the battleship *Vittorio Veneto*, were still at anchor. They always were. Early one morning, while I was flying this mission, it occurred to me that some years before the outbreak of war, while riding my motorcycle from Coventry to my home in Leicester, I had stopped in Hinckley to see a moving picture staring Errol Flynn and David Niven entitled *Dawn Patrol*. At the time I saw the picture I could never have imagined in my wildest dreams that I would someday in the near future find myself, as I was doing now, actually flying the 'Dawn Patrol', for real, while Errol Flynn and David Niven had only been play-acting to make a moving picture. I felt sure that they were paid a lot more than the 10s. 6d (52.5p) a day that I was supposedly being paid for doing the real thing. Aw! Maybe calling me Wonderboy is OK.

The aircrews were housed in a small mansion in the village of La Marsa. It was too far from the airstrip to walk and the only transport held by 682 Squadron was a 15-hundredweight Dodge pick-up. Colonel Roosevelt lent us a jeep but withdrew it when Sergeant Fletcher failed to give the colonel a lift in it (didn't he know that it was politically incorrect not to give the son of the President of the United States of America a lift?). It should be noted that, although we were part of the Mediterranean Allied Air Forces and under USAAF command, the USAAF were not authorised to supply us with equipment, although Colonel Roosevelt could and did lend me aeroplanes. The RAF did not provide us with any real back up, other than our aeroplanes. When needs must and the devil drives this lack of any ground transport other than a South African 15-hundredweight Dodge pick-up truck moonlight requisitioning opened up on a grand scale. It started when a few non-operating Volkswagen *Kubelwagens* were found in the citrus grove. Knowing that the Germans had left in a hurry, they would certainly have been forced to abandon a number of these vehicles in other places. It did not take much time to organise a systematic air search of the local environs and locate a few. With the aid of the Dodge pick up, many were retrieved and hidden in the citrus grove where they were cannibalised to create operating personal transport. Unfortunately, for some reason, the logistics of the British forces worked in strange ways; for example, only one Merlin kit, comprised mostly of flimsy pressed-steel spanners, was issued to each squadron while the United States provided a complete set of wonderful 'Snap-On' tools with every spare engine, but they did not fit the fasteners used on British aircraft. In Britain I was accustomed to using bicycles to get to the dispersals where the aeroplanes were parked, but in La Marsa there were no bicycles and British Military Police were told to confiscate any vehicles such as our *Kubelwagens* whenever they were encountered. When this happened, we would merely find our way back to La Marsa, which was out of the jurisdiction of the British military police and pull another *Kubelwagen* out from the citrus grove wondering 'What a way to run a war'. We could have an aeroplane but not a way of getting to it. But at least we were given aeroplanes? But it might have been difficult to do our job without, and sometimes with, them.

Although such activities were a respite from the true act of war, it did make the absurdity of war more tolerable, but the Gremlins were still up to their tricks. Although I personally did not cause any damage to any aircraft, other pilots had minor mishaps. Nothing had happened that compromised the operations of the squadron, but the squadron commander called a meeting and stated that in the future any pilot who caused any damage to an aircraft no matter what the circumstances would be subjected to a court martial. The next day a pilot returning from a maximum-range sortie realised that he would not be able to stop after touchdown and, rather than risk damage to his aircraft, tried to go around for another approach. He did not have enough fuel and spun in, resulting in his death and the loss of an aeroplane. Although graveyard humour, I wondered if he would have been court martialled had he survived.

But do you get a pat on the back when you've beaten the
odds? Like on this sortie to the south of France?

The Gremlins were making their presence fully known. The first sortie that I flew from La Marsa was in a Spitfire Mk IV that I had ferried from Algiers to Mason Blanche. The sortie was to cover targets in the south of France and included Marseilles and Toulon. It being a maximum-range sortie, it necessitated landing at Bone on the Mediterranean coast to top off the fuel tanks. Bone was closer to Algiers but beyond where fighting still continued. After landing at Bone, I realised I had my 'stupid hat' on as I had flown the plane from La Marsa to Bone at low altitude without the need for oxygen. Oxygen was essential to fly at the high altitude required by this operation and I was without an oxygen tube to deliver it. Fortunately, some kind soul lent one to me with my promise to return it when I stopped to obtain fuel on my way back to La Marsa. Whilst refuelling at Bone an American pilot tried to talk me into letting him fly my Spitfire; in return I could fly his P-40 Tomahawk. It seemed difficult for the easygoing American lieutenant to understand that Royal Air Force pilots did not have the discretion to let someone else fly their aeroplanes and certainly not one engaged in a combat operation. After take off from Bone I crossed the Mediterranean and started to make the photographic run along the docks at Marseilles when the dreaded Gremlins decided to intervene – the engine stopped.

Without power I started losing altitude from the 28,000 feet I was flying at but continued the photographic run of the docks while trying to restart the engine. After kicking the aircraft round to the left and following the line of the docks which put me on a westerly course toward the flat land of the Rhone delta and the Spanish border, I made the decision that if I was unable to restart the engine I would glide to a remote area where I would either bale out or put the aircraft down. Although I felt calm, I was concerned that my attempts to restart the engine were not meeting with success, until at 17,000 feet the engine coughed and, after a few more tries, started. I was relieved as it once again provided the smooth powerful roar of the Rolls Royce Merlin engine and I was able to climb back to altitude and continue covering the targets of Toulon and Buere-sur-Rhône in the south of France without the fear of becoming a guest of the German government. At Buere-sur-Rhône, I could see some naval units turning in tight circles; perhaps they thought that I was going to throw my Dalton computer at them.

The return flight across the Mediterranean was uneventful and the fuel gauges indicated that there was enough fuel for me to return to La Marsa without having to land at Bone. Wrong, the fuel gauges lied and, with the engine dying, I had to attempt an emergency landing while I still had some choice of a place to land. The trouble was I was near Mateur in an area where I understood fighting was still continuing and had no idea of which side of the line I might be on. But I had no option but to land. Lining up on a flat area, I decided to extend the undercarriage and possibly avoid damage to the aircraft in case it might be in friendly territory. As the ground sped by, I was confronted by wires extended across my flight path but managed to pull up over them and rapidly sank to the ground. Although the touchdown was less than desirable, the ground appeared solid and covered in coarse vegetation but, as I slowed to a stop, the right wing went down. I thought the right undercarriage had collapsed. I climbed out of the aircraft and prepared to destroy it in the event I was in German-held territory. Due to the fuel tanks being empty, I was wondering how to set fire to the machine when a few men wearing westernised Arab clothes appeared. They did not behave in a threatening manner and went to look at the aeroplane. That was when I realised that the undercarriage was undamaged: the aircraft had come to a stop, the right wheel had run into a hole, the wing-tip was a few inches above the ground and there was no damage.

Not knowing any Arabic and hoping that they might understand French I tried to indicate that I did not have any 'Essence' but was unable to ask if there were any Germans around. They obviously understood that I was out of fuel and went away. I removed the camera magazines and continued preparing to destroy the aircraft should Germans turn up. The magazines would have been of no use to the Germans, but if I did not have to destroy the aircraft I might still be able to deliver them to photographic intelligence. I was taken by surprise when the men not only returned but were accompanied by members of what I took to be the US forces, but they did not speak English. After lifting the aircraft wing up and putting the wheel on level ground, they brought a 50-gallon drum of fuel and pumped the petrol into the main fuel tank.

With no knowledge of the fuel's octane rating, other than it smelt right, I thought that if the engine would start it might be possible to fly the aeroplane out of there. Due to the many holes in the ground I was unable to find a straight line that was long enough for lift off. The only way that I could find a distance great enough was with a dog leg. By driving a stick into the ground and attaching my handkerchief to provide a visible marker at the point where I could kick in left rudder to a slightly different heading and using a bush to aim at, I thought that I might be able to get the aircraft airborne. Anyway it was worth a try. After replacing the magazines on the cameras and climbing into the cockpit, I set about starting the engine. Although the priming pump became solid and pumped fuel, when I pressed the starter and boost buttons the engine turned over but did not start. I felt devastated that, having overcome all the problems of this ill-fated trip, if

I was unable to overcome this last remaining setback I would not be able to redeem myself and finish the operation successfully. The battery was almost drained, I had almost pulled the iron out of the fire and now kicked myself for my stupidity – I had failed to turn the ignition switches on. With my fingers crossed, I pressed the starter once again. To my surprise and joy, the engine fired up. Without any engine checks I opened the throttle and, as my speed increased, I kicked in rudder at the handkerchief and felt the controls coming alive and was elated to see the ground fall away.

Turning back over the gathering of men, I saluted them; they were laughing and waving and, although I was unable to tell just who they were, I thanked them in the only way I could, by waggling my wings as I flew overhead breathing a deep sigh of relief. I had been lucky enough to overcome all the things that had gone wrong and even the mistake of not landing at Bone to refuel; the only other problems were being late and suffering heart failure. The engine ran smoothly for the rest of the flight back to La Marsa and I had a deep feeling of relief as I passed over the Roman aqueduct north of Tunis. Landing at La Marsa it was with thanks that, although the Gremlins had done their worst, I had still had managed to finish the operation successfully. However, it was not an operation that I would care to repeat and I had forgotten to return the oxygen tube I had borrowed at Bone; they are probably still waiting for it.

The operation deserved the award of a DFC (Distinguished Flying Cross) but the Gremlins had the last laugh. I was told from the initial plot of the photographs that I had missed the targets, although the final plot made some days later showed that I had flown right down the centre of the targets but that the cameras had been set with a 10 per cent gap in the middle instead of a 10 per cent overlap, something that I could neither be aware of nor be blamed for. By then any possibility of a DFC was forgotten – those damned Gremlins had the last laugh. On 10 August 1943 the squadron adjutant, Flight Lieutenant Johnson, called me into the office and told me that I would be awarded the United States Army Air Forces Air Medal for having completed more than five successful missions for the USAAF. Like the DFC, the Air Medal never materialised either.

I guess I was not the right type to receive any recognition or decorations. The fevers and high temperatures were not diminishing and did not add to my feeling of well being.

At high altitude the authoritative roar of the Merlin engine was reduced to a quiet purr so that the long crossings of the Mediterranean in the rarefied atmosphere made it easier to occupy my mind by listening to imaginary classical music, although Richard Addinsel's 'Warsaw Concerto' was my favourite piece at the time – not an epoch-making observation and hardly a departure from normality.

My volunteering for service in the Royal Air Force had led to a position fraught with danger and I loved it. I had been elevated to the status of a commissioned officer and was promoted from pilot officer to the next higher rank of flying officer which, to some extent, compensated for the moments of dire terror that I had felt from time to time. As a soldier in the Army it might have been a lot less stressful. But I had one regret. At the time Flying Officer Cline left me stranded in Gibraltar with the feeling that I had been treated with contempt by an officer because I was nothing but a lowly sergeant, I now found that at the time that happened I had been of equal rank to Cline, they had just neglected to inform me that I had in fact been a commissioned as an officer since 3 February 1943. Oh, if I had only known – I would have kicked that *!#*^d in the – you know where. Although Harry Cline and I got along afterwards, I never brought up the Gibraltar event; it just seemed best to let sleeping dogs lie, but I was still angry. An apology, recognition and thanks would have been nice.

Avoiding being shot down by the enemy is one thing but how do you avoid getting killed by things like this?

Flying in many aircraft that were not airworthy or were inappropriate for the operation together with failure of equipment was beginning to seem to be normal. After flying from Algiers to the west coast of Italy and having covered some 200 miles of coast line with my cameras indicating that they were working, it turned out that they were not. With all that risk for nothing, I was beginning to wonder if it was not just the enemy who was trying to kill me. It appeared that my own government might be intent on accomplishing what the enemy had failed to do – so far. Not feeling good and having frequent temperatures of over 105F degrees, together with night sweats and a marked loss of weight, I reported these problems to a medical officer, together with the irrational phobia I had when flying across the Mediterranean at high altitude. No notice appeared to be made of my condition or treatment provided. Having no previous experience with ill health, other than the painful experience of tonsillitis as a child, I assumed that all personnel probably had similar problems and I should just try to ignore them. But the onset of depression was accelerated and triggered by an assignment to cover targets in the Marseilles and Toulon area; I was unable to get the aircraft (Spitfire BP920) to climb above 17,000 feet as I flew up the west coast of Sardinia. Trying to cover the targets at that altitude would have been impossible and, although halfway to the targets, I decided discretion was the better part of valour and returned to La Marsa. During the return flight, remembering the criticism that had been made when I was unable to get that wreck of an aircraft above 17,000 feet over La Maddalena, I knew I was in trouble again. After parking the aircraft, Flying Officer Sims, the engineering officer, who happened to be at the airstrip came to the aeroplane and climbed onto the wing before I left the cockpit and asked what the problem was. Thinking that he was referring to the reason for my early return, I told him of my inability to obtain the required altitude. The engineering officer pointed out that on that aircraft, and only that aircraft, the control for the filter used to prevent the ingress of sand on take off as used on aircraft in the North African theatre was operated by a lever down on the left-hand side of the pilot's seat and not next to the fuel selectors where it was located on all the other Spitfires in the squadron. Naturally, I felt like an idiot, knowing that if you failed to open the air filter after take off the aircraft would not be able to provide full power. Although this oversight was due to me not having familiarised myself sufficiently with the aeroplane, it certainly would not be accepted as a reason for aborting the operation and I was, as usual, in serious trouble. But Flying Officer Sims said, 'Johnny, don't say anything about the filter just get out of the aeroplane and look at the underside.' The entire underside of the aircraft was covered in black oil; an oil line had burst and only a half gallon from the fourteen gallons of oil onboard at take off remained. Aborting an operation with a problem like this was acceptable but what worried me was that I had not returned for that reason; there was no way I could become aware of the oil leak until the oil temperature would start to rise together with a drop in oil pressure that would cause the engine to seize and that would have occurred over the target area. It made me feel sick that my return to base had been due to my own ineptitude; it had just been luck that I had turned back for the wrong reason. I hated to think of what would have happened if I had known about the air filter and opened it after take off. I would have carried on to the target with the resulting engine failure. The real reason for returning being known only to Flying Officer Sims and myself relieved me of any repercussions, but I felt weak at the knees when I realised that if I had displayed a stiff upper lip and continued to the target, engine failure would have caused me to become just another casualty of the war. Having unreliable aeroplanes and realising what would have happened, together with all of the other things that had gone wrong during the time that I had been on 682 Squadron, made me wonder if these experiences were typical of all pilots, or had the Gremlins just focused their attention on me and were giving me more than the lion's share? But fate had decreed that I survived where so many had simply disappeared into the Mediterranean. The popular Flight Lieutenant Walker disappeared over Sicily; Flying Officer Woodward, who had been my roommate, had been trained in Rhodesia and did not want to return to England until the war was over. He didn't return. He disappeared without trace into the Mediterranean. It made me wonder if their fate was due to the enemy, or to faulty equipment.

I was happy that the Gremlins had pointed the fickle finger of fate at me and failed. I felt proud of being an operational pilot. Losses that had occurred since I became an operational pilot in 543 Squadron were worrying. The Squadron was disbanded, leaving only Jacky Dearden and me as the sole remaining pilots of A Flight. Although the odds of survival did not seem particularly favourable, if it was my fate to fall victim to the Grim Reaper, surely it had to be at the hands of the enemy. But who cares when you are having 'fun'?

My sense of humour may have been at a low ebb, but at least a sense of humour was apparently alive and well with some in England, although I had strong cause to suspect it was skulduggery rather than humour. War takes on a curious slant when stupidity prevails, the results belonging more on a vaudeville theatre stage, when a simple questionable 'error' of a bookkeeper in London could have such far-reaching effects that even the background of war can provide situations that are so ridiculous they are funny, so here we go:

Who said war was to defend your country?

I was called into the office of the squadron commander and informed by him that I had committed the court-martial offence of overdrawing my bank account. Here we go again, why not accuse me of robbing a bank in China? Surely this had to be a joke. I did not even know I had a bank account. Only rich people had those and I was not one of them. Overdrawing a bank account that I did not know I even had, let alone be able to overdraw it in a place like North Africa was in itself hilarious. So how would I be able to defend myself at a court martial on charges that I had overdrawn a bank account that I didn't even know existed and was a thousand miles away from in North Africa? I guess they did not know I was fighting a war but they couldn't sentence me to Dartmoor while I was in North Africa so I was told by Colonel Roosevelt to fly the B-17 to England and either face a court martial or straighten it out. Who me? What could I do about it? I was a pilot, not an accountant and how, could I solve a problem of which I had no knowledge whatsoever? Does an overdrawn bank account have precedence over bringing the war to a close? So I was given a holiday from the war, courtesy of Colonel Roosevelt, and I flew to England as co-pilot of the B-17 'Mudhen' (see plate 15). Now this is funny: I was enrolled in the British Royal Air Force and about to fly as co-pilot of a United States Army Air Forces four-engine bomber to try to explain away a court-martial offence in England. Of course, the cost was of no importance. Someone thought it more important to find me guilty of something than for me to fight a war.

Boarding the aircraft, Colonel Drue asked me where the twenty United States Army Air Forces enlisted personnel wearing their number-one uniforms and waiting to board the 'Mudhen' were going. I knew *where* they were going but did not know *why*. The colonel then asked a sergeant where he was going. The sergeant replied, 'To London on R and R.' The colonel asked 'Do you have enough money?' The sergeant replied in the affirmative and the colonel merely responded by saying 'have a good time.' This was certainly not the Royal Air Force. But I was in the Royal Air Force on my way to England where regulations made it an offence to wear tropical uniform. I had a *Catch 22* problem: I had nothing but a tropical uniform; I had been commissioned in the field and had only regular enlisted men's khaki uniform and an American officer's shirt. To the Americans common sense would prevail but common sense was not a strong suit in the British military and I was already accused of overdrawing a bank account that I did not even know existed. What a war! It is safe to assume that whoever scripted this sequence of the war had no involvement in operations against the enemy but might well have been suited for a future in Hollywood, while I should probably have been playing a more contributory role in the war as a private in the Army peeling potatoes. With our aircraft loaded we flew to Gibraltar, refuelled and set course for England. It was an opportunity to practise our aircraft recognition skills. We made twenty-seven sightings of other aircraft, some of which were Allied aircraft and some were unidentifiable, but some were German.

Apparently the German aircrews were not practising aircraft recognition that day, which was fortunate as, despite all the machine guns we carried, we did not have even one round of ammunition. The flight from Gibraltar to England provided a little physical exercise as the autopilot did not work and we flew the aeroplane manually the entire way. The B-17 was a big aeroplane and at low altitude took a lot of muscle power to control. With a sigh of relief, we landed at St Mawgan airfield in Cornwall where HM Customs and Excise inspected the plane and failed to find any dutiable items. I thought that they probably did not look very hard because, with the aid of the Americans I had been able to convert the Banque d'Algerie 1,000-franc notes that I had obtained by selling the gold Louis in Algiers into Gibraltar pounds and from those into pounds sterling, since I had no money; all I had was an overdrawn bank account. Customs did not find the Omega wristwatches that I had used some of my ill-gotten money for. I had bought the prestigious Omega wristwatches for £5 each after their circuitous route from Switzerland to Tangier and then to Gibraltar by way of Algeciras. I intended to sell half of the watches at £10 each (which in England was a giveaway price) to recover my cost and give the other half to aircrew members to replace their non-existent navigators' watches. No one I knew had ever seen a navigator's watch and it was somewhat of a challenge to navigate without a timepiece. I do not recall ever seeing a timepiece, even in British aircraft, that had a mounting for one. But the bananas I brought back from Gibraltar brought a few smiles when I gave the now rare fruit away. The cloud ceiling was low on the leg between St Mawgan and Mount Farm and, as we flew past the steeple of Wells Cathedral at low altitude, it felt good to be back in England. At the USAAF base at Mount Farm I was still wearing tropical khaki uniform because I did not have an officer's blue uniform. The tropical uniform I was wearing was against regulations in England. I was in enough trouble already, so how could I get out of this?

Events had almost made me forget that, before my sudden departure to North Africa, I had been measured for officers' uniforms at the Sheppard and Woodward tailors on the 'High' in Oxford, but that was a lifetime ago and I had almost forgotten about them due to other pressing matters. But Oxford was twelve miles away from Mount Farm and I did not know if the uniforms had even been made. The Americans always seemed to have a way of meeting the objective, military regulations or not; they drove me to the tailors who checked their records and found that they had indeed made the uniforms and put them in storage because I had not claimed them. They were able to retrieve the uniforms from storage in just a few minutes and changed the rank insignia from pilot officer to my current rank of flying officer. I donned the uniform and felt strange wearing the blue uniform of a Royal Air Force officer. I felt like an impostor playing a part in which I did not belong. I don't know how, or if, the tailors were paid because I was not presented with a bill. The only money I had was what I had brought from Tunisia and without that I would have been destitute. I felt self-conscious, it being the first time I had been in England as a Royal Air Force officer. The Americans drove me to RAF Station Benson (where previously my rank had been that of sergeant) and now I was being saluted at the gate. Entering the officers' mess at this formal RAF station I had a feeling of not belonging, although this was quickly dispelled by the friendliness of the officers, of whom I was now one. When awakened the following morning by a member of the WAAF bearing a cup of tea, I thought that I had been sent to Heaven. It was frosting on the cake to find that Jacky Dearden was also an officer and operating with 541 Squadron; it appeared that the RAF Form 1020a applications for commissions had in fact been unbelievably effective. My only regret was that I was not also operating from Benson, over northern Europe, where, if anything untoward were to happen to me, at least it would be in the skies where I felt I belonged.

But back to the story of why I was in England. First, although I had been in the presence of so many well-known people while in North Africa, it was still a surprise when Lord Nuffield visited the officers' mess and, in the company of a few other officers, bought me a drink. Lord Nuffield was a benefactor to Royal Air Force aircrews; when they were on leave he provided them with 10 shillings (50p) a day, which was paid in addition to the airman's RAF pay. A hotel was also provided for their use in Torquay with no charge. Lord Nuffield, the former Mr Morris, was the manufacturer of Morris cars and MG (Morris Garages) sports cars and at his Cowley factory near Oxford was currently modifying Spitfires to incorporate pressurised cockpits. I was awed that a person from my lowly beginnings had in such a short time met the President of the United States's son, Elliot Roosevelt (my commanding officer in North Africa), and now Lord Nuffield, in addition to Lord Malcolm Douglas Hamilton, among many others. In my wildest dreams it would never have occurred to me that I would even see such people let alone talk with them, but that was one of the fortunes of war and all this was happening because, instead of flying operations in the Mediterranean theatre, I was accomplishing the awesome task of trying to straighten out a bank account I didn't know existed.

It may seem reprehensible that the only funds I had were obtained in such a subversive manner, but was it any less reprehensible that for several months they had neglected to pay me as a sergeant or even make me aware that I was an officer and that my pay was being 'accidentally' purloined from a bank account that I did not know existed? I had no shame in using the funds that had resulted from my entrepreneurial affair with the gold Louis in Algiers; without them I would have had nothing. My 'bank account' was overdrawn and I had not received any pay that I knew of for months. I did not even know how to use what transpired to be a chequing account, or the mysteries of using cheques with a requirement to place your signature across a two-penny stamp! That was something that only officers and professional people who had chequing accounts would know about. With no knowledge of those mysteries, I was expected to sort out and solve the mystery of an overdrawn bank account. I was just a pilot and, with a war going on, was supposed to be fighting the enemy, not some Whitehall accounting bookkeeper. There I go losing my sense of humour again.

I was enjoying this respite from the war and enjoying the uplift of having become a Royal Air Force officer. It is funny to think that they brought me all the way from Africa to solve the mystery of an overdrawn bank account; after all if the bank couldn't sort it out why did they think I could. I had been over a thousand miles away, so let's just get on with the court martial; at least in prison I would survive the war, if not this foolishness. How could I try to explain that I was overseas in a place where I could not even access a bank account, even if I knew that I had one, and that should have been obvious? How could I overdraw a bank account I did not know I had? Why was the onus on me to explain the overdrawn bank account? Surely it was up to the bank to explain to me how the account had been overdrawn, together with an apology for their ineptitude while I was in the middle of a war in the North African theatre. With the feeling that it would seem obvious to anyone that I could not have accessed the account, why was I threatened with a court martial? All I could do was plead insanity and throw myself on the mercy of the court.

I arrived at the office of the Lloyds Cox's and King's Branch bank just a few hundred feet from Trafalgar Square to be appraised of the irregularities of my irresponsible handling of the bank account at the branch 'responsible' for administering the accounts of RAF officers. After insisting someone examine the books, they arrived at a conclusion: first – yes, there is an account in the name of Flying Officer Kenneth B. Johnson, serial number 143663, and it is overdrawn. However, it appeared that some irregularities 'may' have occurred resulting in incorrect entries: a bookkeeper was crediting my pay to the name of the next officer on the *Air Force List*, an officer by the name of Kelly. Another irregularity in the entries was also noted: the bookkeeper was also deducting debits made by that officer from the zero balance of my account that had resulted in my having committed a court martial offence. I was a pilot, not a bookkeeper, and wondered how such glaring incorrect entries could go unobserved and require me to fly a four-engine bomber all the way from Africa to bring the matter to a head. I wondered who belonged in Dartmoor? Kelly, the accountant, or me? No, we all belonged in an insane asylum, but perhaps that is where we were already!

I wondered why all that expenditure had been made and my future put in jeopardy and it being considered necessary for me to be present in London while someone looked at the books to see if any mistakes had been made – mistakes that were so glaringly obvious. But the account was 'straightened out' and I was cleared of any potential court-martial charges. The mad mad world of authoritarian vaudeville had created a scenario of someone fighting a war overseas unaware that he had been promoted to commissioned rank with a bank account opened in his name and would have to leave a theatre of operations, spending all these resources because of some lowly civilian bookkeeper in England who, it appeared, either could not read or add or subtract correctly – with no oversight? Gilbert and Sullivan had made comic operas on less material than this. Who said there is no humour in war. If William Shakespeare had had this information, it might well have been the subject of *A Comedy of Errors*.

Conscription into the Army as a private would have been poetic justice for the accountant, or was hanging the punishment for sabotaging the war effort? But be that as it may, I was never aware of my account ever being credited with the several months' pay that Kelly had received. I wonder why Kelly was never aware of these irregularities, or was he oversees and unaware of the irregularities too?

With the conclusion of this comedy and the mystery of the money missing from my bank account being solved, I was left with an unblemished financial background and a bank account with no money. I could not help wondering why I had still lost and who got the money?

I am back in England and even my mother
does not recognise me

I was given leave and informed that I would be contacted when further orders became available. Together with another flying officer by the name of Irwin, I flew to Braunstone aerodrome in a Tiger Moth where I was dropped off and Flying Officer Irwin flew the aircraft back to Benson. Crossing the road to the Airman's Rest public house, I was fortunate enough to obtain a ride into Leicester where I caught the bus from Humberstone Gate to Catherine Street, just a short walk to my mother's house on Shetland Road. Although the key was hanging in its usual place in the front porch, there was no one home. When my mother returned from shopping in the Leicester Market, she said she had seen me in Humberstone Gate but did not think it could be me as she knew I was overseas and, in any case, I was not an officer. Oh well, with no telephones there was no way she could have known, but that's life in the fast lane. Naturally Tony Scott was home but where was Sid Johnson? Tony was home on survivor's leave; his tanker had been en route to England when it had been torpedoed and lost. Survivors, including Tony, had been picked up by the Royal Navy's HM Trawler *Firefly* that was en route to St John's, Newfoundland, but this vessel was also torpedoed and sank. Fortunately, the surviving crew members were picked up by yet another vessel en route to England and eventually arrived safely in port. This entitled Tony to thirty days' survivor's leave. Tony had the word that Sid would be arriving at the LMS Station on London Road on the train from Peterborough due at 9:00pm the following evening. Sid, who had completed his course on Hotspur training gliders, was now a sergeant being trained to fly the troop-carrying Horsa glider.

It's the middle of a war – and nice things happen?

The following evening Tony and I went to the Grand Hotel Bar on Belvoir Street to while away the time until Sid's train would arrive and struck up a conversation with a sergeant in the United States Army by the name of Furey. The three of us went to pick up Sid from the railway station in my Morris Ten car. It was a dark night and in the blackout we did not see Sid, but a girl wearing the uniform of the Auxiliary Territorial Service (ATS) asked Tony, who was wearing the uniform of a ship's officer, if he were a taxi driver. After all, in the dark Tony did look a bit like a taxi driver and, realising that Sid had not been on the train, he replied that he was not, but knowing that the bus services had stopped at 9:00pm he offered her a lift. We drove the young lady to her home in the village of Birstall just outside Leicester and were happy to have helped a fellow member of the military service. The pubs being closed, we dropped Sergeant Furey off where he requested. He had been a fun guy to talk with and we arranged to meet him again the following evening. The next day Sid showed up with some excuse about why he had missed the train the night before and the three of us set off to meet Sergeant Furey as arranged at the Grand Hotel bar, but he didn't show up.

A few years later Tony was in a bar on 42nd Street in New York city when he saw a US Army captain who looked familiar and could hardly believe the coincidence when he found that it was Sergeant Furey who had been promoted to commissioned rank. Now, if that coincidence was not enough, Captain Furey insisted that Tony accompany him to his home in the Bronx and meet his wife. The reason for not turning up at the Grand Hotel bar that night was revealed; he had made a date with the ATS girl whom we had taken home to Birstall and she was now his wife and living in the USA. That is how Tony came to be known as Cupid and I was referred to as Eros. But, in the cavalier days of the Second World War, Sid and I felt that Tony should have been given twice that amount of survival leave since he had survived two ships being sunk, even if it was on one crossing, although this was a sort of gallows humour: although the events were tragic, it was one way to keep a sense of optimism. It would have been uplifting if we could have known what the future had held for the chance meeting of Sergeant Furey and the ATS girl.

There were times when it was difficult to keep a stiff upper lip. My mother gave me the bad news that, while I was in Africa, a German bomber had dropped a bomb in front of my Uncle Will's home in Sneinton Dale, Nottingham. It had killed my cousin, who was also named Ken. Ken Allen, the son of Will Allen, the former well-known captain of Nottinghamshire Cricket Club, had been a student at the prestigious Mundella School in Nottingham and had been awaiting induction into the Royal Air Force where he had been accepted for pilot training. I was not only sad but when my mother told me that the funeral cortege had been machine-gunned by a German aircraft I became very angry and for a few days wished I could get my hands on an aeroplane and give the Germans back in kind. I calmed down when rationality returned, knowing that the German pilot could not have known what he was shooting at; it was just another ugly incident highlighting the stupidity of war.

I wondered how my mother could be so stoical, the way she had maintained her steadfastness with the impact that two world wars had had on her and were still having, sitting in the little Anderson air-raid shelter in the back garden of our home on Shetland Road listening to the scream of bombs as they passed overhead with the flashes as they exploded penetrating into the darkness of our shelter. I knew that she must be terrified and was glad that in the darkness she could not see that I, too, was terrified. Some of the bombs fell close by and, although I had been in many bombing raids, these bombs had fallen so close to my home that it was really scary. It was strange having to live with bombs falling; sometimes I had watched dispassionately as they fell since there was nothing that I could do about it; you were defenceless on the ground. At least in the air it was possible to take evasive action if you saw danger approaching.

One evening as the light was starting to fade, a German bomber dropped a type of bomb referred to as a land-mine (a bomb modified from German naval ordnance), attached to a parachute and, from the front gate of my home on Shetland Road, Leicester, I watched it descend slowly. It drifted gently to the north-west, landing on a housing estate on the far side of Blackbird Road where it detonated, killing eighty people.

The inevitable knock on the door came, and a police constable passed the message along that I was to telephone Group Captain Lord at the Air Ministry. This I did to be informed that I was to report back to RAF Benson immediately. I arrived at the LMS Station in Leicester to catch the next train to London en route to Benson. Problem – the train arriving on platform 3 was so packed that I had to request assistance to find space. Naturally the platform attendant did not believe the urgency of my request and I had to force myself into a corridor and literally stand on one foot for several minutes. The train left Leicester for London at midnight, making it an overnight journey. When I arrived at Benson I was rather tired and my hopes of remaining in England and being posted back to operational flying were shattered when I was again ordered to fly a PRU Spitfire to an overseas location. After a little rest, I test flew the aircraft and was given instructions to deliver it to 682 Squadron at La Marsa. After picking up a parachute, flying helmet, oxygen mask etc. that I needed to fly the aircraft, together with other items such as badges of rank, pilot's wings and an assortment of things not available in the field that I was asked to take with me, I also included a few newspapers for good measure to give others a taste of home.

The following morning I took off on the first leg of the flight to deliver the aircraft to 682 Squadron at La Marsa in Tunisia. The flight was not uneventful; I was forced to climb and lose contact with the ground due to a layer of cloud obscuring Dartmoor. This in itself was not a problem and, after clearing the high ground of Dartmoor, I started to descend to regain contact with the ground. Flying the aircraft on instruments in the thick cloud as I lost altitude I was feeling comfortable but annoyed that I had fallen into the trap of being sent overseas again and wished that I had volunteered to be sent overseas in the first place. Had I volunteered for a posting as far away as possible, they would probably have stationed me next door to home; it certainly seemed to work that way. All such thoughts were instantly wiped from my mind as the wheel of an American B-24 bomber came hurtling past my cockpit at a closing speed of over 300 mph. Instantly I pushed the control column forward and the wheel missed the top of my canopy by no more than a few feet. With a dry mouth, I broke out of the base of the cloud and realised what had happened. I was directly in line with a runway at RAF Station St Eval. The B-24 must have just taken off and climbed into the low cloud. I wondered if this was the harbinger of things to come – it was! Although informed that I was to take the aeroplane to La Marsa airfield outside Tunis by way of Gibraltar and Ras el Ma in Morocco, the weather forecast precluded a flight until the following day. I filled the evening by watching the film *Random Harvest* on the screen of a small cinema on the first floor of a building in Redruth. The next day my mood matched the weather, dull and raining; there did not seem to be any urgency to get the aircraft to La Marsa and there appeared no reason why they needed to spring this on me without any notice. It was always hurry up and wait. Here I was on my way back to Africa; was this the way of those people who ruled my wretched fate in their nice safe and secure offices for some reason punishing me? After all, it was Jack Dearden who had volunteered for overseas service, not me, and Jack was still in England. My past performance had been outstanding; I had never missed a single target, and surely my performance would have been sufficient to ensure my continuing to operate over targets in the northern European theatre? Or did they not think that was dangerous enough for me? Heck, I had even been told by intelligence at the Central Interpretation Unit that one of my operational photographs had disclosed a U-boat factory and launching facility near Lubeck that they did not know about, together with much more important intelligence.

What do you do when you are at 28,000 feet and hundreds of miles from nowhere – totally lost?

With these misgivings I attended the pre-flight briefing with twin-engine Lockheed Hudson aircraft crews the evening before the flight to Gibraltar. After the general briefing navigators were told they were to remain for the navigational briefing; this included me since I had to navigate my own aircraft. After the meeting the navigator of a Hudson bomber asked me why I, a pilot, was attending a meeting for navigators and laughed at my reply when I told him I would fly a Spitfire to Gibraltar. Everyone 'knew' a Spitfire did not have the range to make such a flight. At 3:30am next day I went to my aircraft and made the checks ensuring that it would be ready for flight by 6:30am. Leaving the ground crew to finish preparing my aircraft and top up the fuel tanks I left to have breakfast. It was a cold Cornish morning and I had the foresight to wear the shirt and shorts of a tropical uniform under my regular blue uniform knowing that it would be warm when I landed at Gibraltar. Breakfast over, it was time for departure.

After the preliminaries I taxied to the threshold in the miserable rain. The glowering low clouds of the dark grey sky hanging over the runway seemed threatening as I started my take-off roll. In the half-light of dawn, I opened the throttle and increased speed down the runway towards the cliffs that overlooked the sea. Roosting seagulls made me realise that I was taking off on the wrong runway, but it was too late to avoid them as they took flight and my windscreen became opaque with the remains of the unfortunate seagulls. As I passed over the cliffs and moved my left hand to the control column to retract the undercarriage with my right hand, the throttle closed. The ground crew had loosened the throttle friction nut. I should have noticed this and tightened it before take off, but I didn't.

Now the angry sea was reaching up to claim me. I could not see through the windscreen and all I could do was leave the undercarriage down, open the throttle with my left hand and climb to a safe altitude hoping that the engine would not overheat due to the radiators being blanked off by the undercarriage slipstream. I hoped that no one was watching what was happening as I held the control column between my knees and, holding the throttle open with my left hand, tightened the throttle friction nut with my right. After that I retracted the undercarriage, breathed a sigh of relief and settled the aircraft to climb through the clouds to reach my optimum cruise altitude of 28,000 feet. With my oxygen demand system turned to 100 per cent, I climbed to high altitude wondering what else could I do wrong? I was soon to find out.

My climb had taken me above cloud covering the Bay of Biscay, which prevented me from getting a fix as I crossed the coast line of Spain. The only land I could see was a range of mountains protruding through the cloud on my port side. I was lost. I was aware that my navigation had been no navigation at all, but why? I then realised that my service revolver was tucked in the inside calf of my left flying boot next to the compass and deflecting it from a correct indication. With the revolver moved away from the compass I realised that the mountains could only be the Pyrenees and decided to fly a south-westerly course across Spain, hoping to find a break in the clouds and obtain a fix, but there was no break in the clouds. I was barely able to see the ground when I made out a set of runways and guessed they were probably those of Lisbon Airport. My guess was correct and my new course brought me to the Bay of Cadiz, which was not obscured by cloud, and where I was supposed to be. I started letting down and, after losing surplus altitude, rounded Point Europa and landed safely at Gibraltar.

It was approximately 08:00am and pleasantly warm as I removed my blue uniform. I was far more comfortable in my tropical shirt and shorts. About 11:30am an RAF Hudson (Q for Queen) landed and taxied to a spot near the hangars; I could not resist standing there to wait for the crew to climb out. The navigator asked me, 'Haven't I seen you somewhere before?' I replied, 'Yes, at the navigators' briefing at Portreath.' The navigator asked how I had managed to get there before them. I enjoyed the humour in replying, 'Easy, I flew a Spitfire, it was faster!' and walked away.

Instead of flying the direct route that was usually used from Gibraltar to Maison Blanche airfield at Algiers I was instructed to fly south across the Straits of Gibraltar past Tangier and turn inland at Rabat and land at Ras el Ma in Morocco. After refuelling I was to carry on to Maison Blanche and then on to La Marsa. Ras el Ma was just a dusty red sand strip outside what appeared to be an Arab village surrounded by abundant vegetation. It did not have any appeal that might induce me to extend my stay and the red sand staining everything convinced me to get underway as quickly as possible. After take off and climbing to a safe altitude, the route took me over the Atlas Mountains and some of the most remote and apparently desolate valleys that I had ever seen. As I approached Algiers, seeing that I had adequate fuel, I decided not to stop at Maison Blanche and continued to La Marsa non-stop where I made an uneventful landing.

Reflecting back, I had been sent back to England because I had 'committed' a court-martial offence by overdrawing a bank account that I did not know I had, and then was told to go and straighten it out – how about turn and turn about? Although not qualified, I was expected to go and do the job of the bookkeeper and straighten out the errors made by that inept (or possibly dishonest) bookkeeper whose job it was in the first place and who was the cause of all these recent happenings. Why not reverse the situation and expect him do my job and have him try and end this stupid war? Perhaps my sense of humour was becoming warped but the war now seemed more of a comedy show than a serious conflict.

The next day I took a Spitfire up for an air test. As I flew low over the citrus grove on final approach my flaps blew up; the rubber seal on the flap-selector switch had ruptured in just the same way as had happened to

Flying Officer Cline at Gibraltar. I immediately returned the flap-selector switch to the 'up' position to preserve pneumatic pressure for the brakes on the short strip but also applied full power in an attempt to go around, but it was too late on the approach to successfully abort and in a three-point attitude I stalled heavily onto the sandy ground. I need not have worried about the brakes because, as I closed the throttle on impact, the aircraft did not even bounce but came to a complete stop in just a few feet – in the soft sand. So all was well that ended well, there being no damage to the aeroplane or the pilot. It would technically be considered a perfect landing. The following day I flew an operation to Sardinia and for once the equipment worked, although the targets hardly seemed worthwhile.

The following day Squadron Leader Morgan told me that I was being sent back to England. I knew it could not be because of an overdrawn bank account and hoped it meant that I was to get back to flying operations over northern Europe again, but a horrible thought crossed my mind. A few weeks earlier a Squadron Leader Stephenson visiting from Benson had made remarks which indicated that some note had been made about my 'attitude' regarding flying over the Mediterranean and commented that I had made a name for myself in England, which implied to me that I was not making a name for myself in North Africa. I had never even thought of avoiding any operation and had flown every operation assigned to me, feeling gratified that I was so effectively contributing to the war effort. Not scheduled to fly, while at the airfield at Maison Blanche just wearing shorts and a light shirt, I was told it was fortunate that I had come to the airfield as they needed a pilot to cover targets in the south of France. Did I baulk? No, with no flying gear I borrowed a flying helmet and oxygen mask and flew the operation dressed only in shirt and shorts. I flew the mission despite the minus 30-degree Fahrenheit temperature at 30,000 feet with no flying clothing, or even gloves. On my return to Maison Blanche after completing the operation successfully, I had difficulty in changing hands to lower the undercarriage and found I could not move my fingers as they were so cold. Despite this I still landed safely. The rest of my body had been in the shade of the cockpit and was so numb that I was unable to climb out of the aircraft without assistance. As the numbness started to wear off, I endured painful pins and needles in my extremities, fingers, and legs as the circulation returned, fortunately without evidence of frostbite. Could any person who would voluntarily undertake such an operation like that and treat it as just another mission be lacking in moral fibre? Were they now, after all the operations that I had flown from the Baltic to the Sahara, insinuating that I was less than desirable? I had coped successfully with many difficulties that other pilots had not experienced and what stung was the deep-down sense of shame that I felt about not being exposed to the danger of operations in the far more dangerous skies of northern Europe. The missions there provided a much greater exposure to the enemy than in this theatre and I had felt gratified in fully accomplishing what I had been trained to do. I had the feeling in England that I was in the right place, actively engaged in defending my country from the continuing bombing attacks that I myself so often had experienced. I had done everything right in North Africa, so why change? It had been confusing to me to be shuttled about, moving from targets in the Baltic to targets in the Mediterranean without warning and accused of unfounded charges, causing me to have to go back to England to answer the absurd accusations. Near misses had shaken me but not reduced my effectiveness, so why could not someone just be honest and tell me why it appeared that there was a cloud over my head?

Chapter 9

Why?

The final insult, although unintended, came when Squadron Leader Morgan informed me that I was scheduled for a maximum-range sortie the following day, 17 August 1943, but told me that I did not need to fly it. I felt angry. Was it not obvious the way I felt about flying every sortie? If I was scheduled to fly it I replied that, of course, I would fly it. The following morning there was thick fog, making it necessary for me to angle the aircraft on the landing strip so that when I advanced the throttle rapidly for take off it gave me room to correct the torque-induced swing and get off the ground in the shortest possible distance. With visibility of only a few feet, getting off the ground in the minimum distance was essential to avoid any hidden obstacles. Although I knew I would not be able to land again until the fog had burned off later in the day, I was not concerned as it would take several hours to cover the targets of Livorno, La Spezia and Genoa before returning. Squadron Leader Morgan, obviously with the best of intentions, wrote that I had begged to fly the operation. When I became aware of that I found the comment irritating; I had volunteered to fly operations in the past but 'beg' to fly one? I flew this one exactly the same as I had flown every operation. Was no one aware of all the operations I had flown without showing any regard about how easy or how dangerous they might be? I thought my dedication was obvious. Surely someone might have noticed that I had successfully covered targets ranging from the Baltic to the Sahara and overcome difficulties that some might not have coped with. Yes, there were times I was scared – wasn't everyone? It was annoying that I was not given any choice; my performance on the squadron had been at least as good as anyone else or perhaps even better. But maybe there was no need for concern; if so, why not be open and tell me up front so that I would know where I stood. It would be nice to know if someone was aware of what I had accomplished. I felt as though I was being treated as incompetent, and that hurt.

WHY?

A summary of my thoughts was that since all the pilots but two, who had been killed in crashes, had disappeared without trace into the Mediterranean, was it unreasonable for me to ask what might have caused the loss of consciousness I had experienced? Frankly, after two interceptions over northern Europe, I felt that if I were to be killed there, at least my family would have some knowledge of what had happened to me in contrast to just disappearing. Surely my dedication to duty was obvious, I flew every operation that I was assigned, plus others that I was not assigned. I never expressed or had any desire to discontinue flying operations until the enemy was defeated and always stated that.

Told that I would be transferred to Hussein Bey, a transit camp near Algiers, en route to England by surface transport and arrive back in Britain either late in the year or early the next year made me feel that my time was of no value and that I was being sidelined when I should be fighting the enemy. When Colonel Roosevelt heard about this he arranged to fly me back to England aboard the 'Mudhen'.

During my time with the NAPRW the colonel had treated me as a competent officer. Perhaps he had been impressed by some of the initiative I had shown, as for example when acting as supply officer of 682 Squadron I had asked him if he could provide me with an aircraft to fly to Algiers to bring back high-pressure cylinders of oxygen, which were needed to continue operation of the high-level Spitfires. There being no high-pressure oxygen available in Tunis, the only way to obtain any was to fly to Algiers and get a cylinder or two. He may have been impressed by my reply when he told me that the only aircraft he had available was a B-25. Although I had never flown a B-25, I said, 'That will do, Sir', and found myself a co-pilot. The B-25, although a first-class aircraft, was designed to carry bombs, not freight, and, although obtaining the cylinders of high-pressure oxygen was easy, loading them into the aircraft was not. Loading them through the rear access hatch I wedged them against the top of the main spar and after tying them in place the problem was solved. Landing on the short strip at La Marsa was exciting; instead of the normal 90 mph approach speed over the threshold, it was necessary to bring the B-25 all the way to touchdown at 135 mph, but I need not have worried. The roll was stopped with plenty of room to spare. Later a B-17 Flying Fortress did not fare so well. As I came in for a landing with a Spitfire, I was surprised to see the B-17 sitting squarely in the middle of the citrus grove at the end of the landing strip. Apparently the pilot had not cycled his brakes after touchdown and when they faded he was unable to stop. Despite the foray into the citrus grove, the aircraft was undamaged.

Colonel Roosevelt was perhaps also pleased by my saving the morale of the USAAF personnel. No facility for making ice cream had yet been set up in the newly-liberated Tunis, and the United States forces seemed to have difficulty operating without such luxuries. To provide a temporary respite from the lack of ice cream, I was asked to fly a fighter from Tunis to Algiers to restore their morale. At Maison Blanche I loaded three 5-gallon containers of ice cream into my aircraft, took off and climbed to 30,000 feet. At that altitude the minus-30-degree temperature kept the ice cream solidly frozen. This solved the ice cream shortage successfully, even though only temporarily, but I liked ice cream too.

It was a sad the day when I boarded the 'Mudhen', the B-17 that Colonel Roosevelt had laid on to fly me back to England. Although cordial relations had existed between the colonel and me, arranging to fly me home overwhelmed me in that he had such consideration. It was something I would never have expected from an RAF officer of similar rank. The third day of September 1943 was not an auspicious day: for the UK, the Second World War had started on that day in 1939 and, on the day of my departure, Wing Commander Ogilvie, visiting La Marsa from No. 681 Squadron, Heliopolis, Egypt, flew an operation to northern Italy in my favourite Spitfire (EN407). He did not return. Of the handful of pilots of 682 Squadron commanded by Squadron Leader Morgan at the time I left, only Sergeants Salmson and Fletcher, together with Sergeant Tetly, who had lost his eyesight in flight but miraculously survived the crash, were left. I have no idea what happened to Flying Officer Cline. Of the nine pilots flying on 682 Squadron Flight Lieutenant Walker, Flying Officer Woodward and Wing Commander Ogilvie had disappeared without trace and two other pilots had been killed in crashes. At the time I left it appeared that of the ten operational pilots who flew on 682 Squadron, four had just disappeared, two were killed in crashes and it seemed that I was one of the remaining four who had survived. I do not recall any other RAF pilots on 682 Squadron in North Africa; perhaps there weren't any.

Although North Africa had been a harrowing experience, it had also been interesting. I had enjoyed exploring Algiers, strolling along the Parisian-style Rue Dislaie and the Rue Michele alongside the Mediterranean and even visited the Kasbah. In the Tunis area, I spent much of my free time around the Bay of Tunis, exploring the ruins at Carthage and the Moorish architecture in the city of Tunis and marvelled at the long Roman aqueduct north of the city.

My association with various members of the United States forces throughout North Africa had been enjoyable and had opened my eyes to the generous attitude they displayed towards everyone. Some of the extra-curricular flying for the USAAF had also been fun. I especially enjoyed flying as co-pilot of General 'Toey' Spaatz's Douglas C-47 Skytrain, known in the RAF as a Dakota, to places like Sousse and Sfax in southern Tunisia at the invitation of Captain Bill Hart USAAF, who hailed from Bismarck, North Dakota. I found its handling characteristics to be well within my capability and felt complimented when he suggested that I move to the United States after the war.

It was gratifying that in La Marsa, the Combined Operations Base in North Africa, I had found himself in the presence of so many famous people including four of President Roosevelt's five sons (Elliot Roosevelt, who was my commanding officer, together with his brothers Frank, John and James), General Alexander, Air Marshal Robb among many others, including Wing Commander Lord Malcolm Douglas Hamilton, my former commanding officer at No. 8 OTU. Wing Commander Lord Malcolm Douglas-Hamilton was always very popular despite his penchant of climbing the highest peak around and insisting that all RAF flying personnel accompany him for the exercise. It was strenuous but enjoyable, although there were still those who termed it punishment rather than fun.

There was also humour displayed at the La Marsa airstrip. Sergeant Tetly was wearing a pith helmet with 'Duty Pilot' lettered on the front and 'Follow Me' stencilled on the back. Air Vice Marshal Robb landed at La Marsa in a Hawker Hurricane and had asked Sergeant Tetly, 'Where is my car?' Tetly replied, 'I am sorry Sir, but a wing commander landed a few minutes ago and I thought the car was for him.' To this, Robb, a jolly type, jokingly commented, 'Well I suppose Air Vice Marshals don't count for much,' at which Sergeant Tetly replied, 'You should bind [seek promotion] for Air Marshal Sir, I'm binding for my crowns [Flight/Sergeant].' Both were still laughing when the Air Vice Marshal's car arrived back. Although I did not like to write entries in my pilot's logbook, even for the operational flights – I was trying to win a war, not write a diary – it was mandatory, and the entries were certified each month, but some pilots did write comments such as funny ditties about operations in their logbooks. One written by Sergeant Sammy Sampson read 'There was St Peter's down in Rome, took one look and turned for home' among the many that were made by pilots. But there was a sombre side when pilots failed to return. When the popular Flight Lieutenant Johnny Walker failed to return from an operation over Sicily, a great deal of time was spent searching for him, but he was never found or heard of again.

With misgivings about being sent home without explanation or option, I boarded the 'Mudhen' for the flight home, first landing at Oran and then on to Gibraltar. After refuelling in Gibraltar and loading a few hands of bananas we took off for St Mawgan airfield in England, but this time with ammunition. Naturally, if you have an umbrella it will not rain and so with the guns loaded no sightings of enemy aircraft were made – not that anyone was disappointed. On the one hand, I was happy to be returning to England and hopefully returning to operations over northern Europe but on the other hand sad at leaving behind the ambience of operating with the free and easy members of the United States forces, but you can't have everything.

My arrival back in England was uneventful and I was sent on leave to await orders. I was anxious to return to operations but felt that the time on leave gave me time to reflect and try to find some rationalisation for the events that had occurred since my enlistment in the Royal Air Force. After the stress of operations in North Africa, I felt relaxed, but the relaxation was tempered by the compelling feeling that I had no right to be relaxing: the war was not over, and I should be flying operations. My record of flying operations in the skies of northern Europe must have been above average since I had been told that I had made a name for myself. Surely I should be flying operations against the enemy, not sitting at home in enforced idleness? While anxiously awaiting orders to return to duty I had the opportunity to help and provide some small contribution to others by giving some of the bananas I had brought back to local heath services; many of the bananas were signed by John Hannah and sold to provide contributions for a local hospital. John Hannah was the youngest aerial winner of the Victoria Cross in the Second World War; after all the crew except the pilot and he had baled out of the badly-damaged and burning Hampden bomber trying to make it back across the North Sea to England, he had managed to put the fire out which enabled Squadron Leader Payne to coach the crippled aircraft back to its base in England. John's modest comment to me was 'What else could I do? My parachute was on fire.' Sadly John died from damage to his lungs in his native Birstall, a mile or two from where I grew up, on 7 June 1947, but the bananas that he autographed helped raise money for the hospital. Apparently bananas that had not been available since the start of the war were now helping sick children since they contained a vitamin that was not otherwise obtainable.

As usual Sid Johnson and Tony Scott had turned up on leave at the same time which helped to lift my spirits in the camaraderie of my two friends. Making the usual fools of ourselves, much to the amusement of the local population, hopefully provided a little humour in the grim reality of war. If our fighting men could laugh about the war, it might make the bombing attacks, suspense and deprivations imposed upon the hardworking civilian population, who were keeping the troops supplied, seem a little more tolerable, but why worry: the war appeared be turning in favour of the Allies.

Chapter 10

OTU Instructor

I received orders to report to No. 8 Operational Training Unit. Whilst not being assigned to an operational squadron was disappointing, it was an appropriate assignment. My primary duties were to train pilots in the transition to PRU Spitfires, be the station test pilot and air-sea-rescue officer, together with various other activities.

Although these activities did not include exposure to enemy action, close shaves and danger still stalked the unwary and accidents were not uncommon. Testing Spitfire AB123, the engine lost power, causing me to make an emergency landing, fortunately without any damage. On another occasion, while spin-testing an aircraft, I was unable to recover but, while preparing to bale out, the aircraft recovered on its own; it probably had a sense of humour. But the most dangerous one was after a test and while on final approach with daylight almost gone. My observer spotted a Mosquito in the dark, also on final and just below us out of sight of each of us pilots. I immediately executed a 360-degree turn to port and avoided the mid-air collision, which would certainly have caused the crews of both aircraft to become another war casualty statistic.

Chapter 11

The End Nears

However, the war in Europe was in its final stages and, with the need for aircrews reducing, I was released from further active duty.

I, together with some of my friends, had survived, but there were many who had not. Titch Beasley was killed when he flew into a mountainside, Charley Chan had been killed flying a Blenheim Mk V in North Africa and Skip Lewis, I was told, had been killed in Malta. These were just a few of my many friends who didn't make it; their names and faces I no longer remember as there were so many of them. I salute them with a feeling of shame for not being able to fly operationally until the war ended. As for Flying Officer Jack Dearden, I lost track of him, but I would suspect that he would have been promoted to flight lieutenant or even squadron leader and return to his home in Ilford when the war ended. I was now twenty-three years of age and needed to recover from the trauma that we and our country had been subjected to. The reward came when VE Day arrived and, at long last, the danger of enemy attacks against the United Kingdom had ended. We could now celebrate victory and give thanks for all the people who had made it possible.

I hoped my wartime service helped the war effort and feel guilty that I was unable to do more. But I had survived the war and had acquired skills that I had never dreamed possible by becoming a skilled pilot, navigator and meteorologist. I hope those heroes whose slipstream I had the privilege of flying in were not too disappointed by my performance.

The End and the Beginning.

Prologue

For those who like to read the end of a book first the following is a list of operations flown during 1942 and 1943. For details it is suggested that you read the book.

RAF Benson, Oxfordshire, England

(The sorties, where applicable, were flown in unarmed aircraft in daylight)

29-11-1942: Flushing, Rotterdam, Holland. Extensive stratus clouds obscured targets.

14-12-1942: Dunkirk, Ostend, Flushing and Low Countries. Covered all targets.

09-01-943: Ostend, Bruges, Ghent, Zeebrugge, Low Countries. Covered all targets.

09-03-1943: Northern France including Cherbourg, Dieppe, Compiègne, etc. Covered all targets.

17-03-1943: Northern France, including Paris, Billancourt, Villacoublay. Covered all Targets.

23-03-1943: Northern France including Caen, Cherbourg. Waiting to complete the last target of Everecy I was intercepted by enemy fighters coming out of the sun; just in time I received an urgent radio warning and managed to escape.

14-04-1943: Low Countries including Zeebrugge, Bruges, Antwerp and other Dutch targets. Covered all targets; however I was intercepted south of the Zuider Zee; fortunately bad weather had come in from the west and I was able to escape by diving into the 18,000 feet of cloud.

PROLOGUE

20-04-1943: Far north-east of Germany including Rostock, Vismar, Warnemünde, Travemünde, Venzendorf, Stade, Cuxhaven etc. Maximum-range sortie across Germany to the border of Poland, complete coverage of all assigned targets was made. Lubeck target revealed unknown U-boat factory, underwater defences at Cuxhaven also revealed. Dark on return to England, completely black with no radio or cockpit lights. Faced with having to either bale out or hopefully land on open ground when I ran out of fuel I miraculously found Benson and landed not knowing if it was on a runway – it was! Admonished for not reporting extra targets covered.

04-05-1943: Western Europe from Portreath, Britain to Gibraltar across Spain and Portugal. I was in formation on F/O Cline who experienced engine failure after crossing into Spain. Despite his not following my instructions on the radio on how to clear his fuel supply problems, I felt dutybound to remain with him to low altitude, leaving us with insufficient fuel to reach Gibraltar. Cline ignored my instructions and tried to fly a direct course to Gibraltar at 1,500 feet but listened to me when I told him on the radio that the cloud that he flew into had a rock lining (Point Europa was 3,500 feet high). Fortunately he listened; after locating him I guided him to a landing on the Rock of Gibraltar where he crashed his aircraft; fortunately no one was injured. The following morning he took my aircraft and finished his journey to Algiers leaving me abandoned on the Rock of Gibraltar.

Flown from Algiers, Algeria, North Africa

Arriving at Maison Blanche, I was informed that I was now a part of the USAAF (United States Army Air Forces) under command of Lt Col Elliot Roosevelt where I flew the following missions:

09-05-1943: Various targets in Sardinia. Covered all targets but the cameras failed to operate.

12-05-1943: Italy, including Bay of Naples, all targets covered but lost consciousness and recovered consciousness not knowing where I was or what I was doing despite 100 per cent oxygen. Eventually my memory returned; fortunately the aircraft was trimmed and still flying straight and level. All targets were covered.

15-05-1943: Targets in the south of France, after being told that it was fortunate that I had come to the airfield as they needed a pilot to fly a sortie.

149

I had no flying gear other than a helmet and oxygen mask and flew the operation wearing only shorts and a shirt for over three hours in minus 30-degree Fahrenheit temperature. After successfully covering all targets, I landed back at Algiers but was so cold I could not move my fingers or climb out of the cockpit unaided. Although no frostbite resulted, the pins and needles as my blood started to circulate was agonising.

16-05-1943: Corsica with targets around Bastia and Civitavecchia in Italy. Had to wait for a B-17 bombing to be completed, my photographs showed a ship still burning.

25-05-1943: Cagliari and targets in Sardinia. Covered all targets.

Flown from La Marsa, Tunisia, North Africa

10-06-1943: South of France, Marseilles, Toulon, and other targets. Experienced engine failure over Marseilles. After losing 10,000 feet, I was able to restart my engine at 17,000 feet. Relying on faulty fuel gauges, I ran out of fuel over Mateur in North Africa where fighting was continuing. I was able to make a successful emergency landing without damage. I could not identify who it was, but fuel was brought to my aircraft and I successfully managed to take off despite fighting reportedly continuing in the area. All targets were covered. Talk of a DFC forgotten as photographs missed targets. I had flown exactly over the middle of the targets, but the cameras had been installed with a gap in the middle.

17-06-1943: Italy, including La Spezia, Livorno and Genoa. Covered all targets.

25-06-1943: Off west coast of Sardinia en route to south of France, a problem with the aircraft caused me to return. I had a leaking oil-line and had only half a gallon left from 14 gallons when I landed. I felt relieved; if I had not turned back my engine would have seized, probably over the target.

19-07-1943: Italy, including Elba and Italian coast line – wasted effort, the cameras were not working again.

22-07-1943: As co-pilot, flew a USAAF B-17 from Gibraltar to St Mawgan, Britain. Twenty-seven sightings of aircraft were made, some of which were Luftwaffe. Fortunately, they did not see us as we had no ammunition for our guns. The purpose of the flight was to sort out the court-martial offence of overdrawing a bank account that I did not know I had.

PROLOGUE

11-08-1943: Ferried Spitfire EN672 from Portreath, England to Gibraltar. Trip uneventful except for navigational difficulties due to fog over both Spain and Portugal.

15-08-1943: Operations over Sardinia. All targets covered.

17-08-1943: Although told I did not need to fly this early morning flight to targets in northern Italy I told the flight commander that since I was scheduled to fly the operation, of course I would fly it and took off at dawn in very thick fog.

3-09-1943: I was told that I was being returned to England, which would take several weeks. Col Elliot Roosevelt laid on the B-17 to take me home. As co-pilot I flew B-17 'Mudhen' from Gibraltar to England, but this time with ammunition. We did not sight any enemy aircraft.

The Rest of the Story

Finding my background did not lend itself to a future in Britain I felt compelled to seek a future overseas and was fortunate enough to be accepted by Canada as an immigrant.

Fate intervened at my first job where I was trying to fix unfixable car engines. The foreman informed me that there was a phone call and, although against company rules, said I should take it as it might be something important. It was: a company was offering me a job – as a pilot. I told them I did not have a pilot's licence. They sent me $100 and told me to get one – I did. The job was flying a Catalina in the North West Territories, doing geophysical surveys. As part of the crew of nine, I earned over $480 for the first week – I was elated; in pounds sterling that was over £100– more than five months' income at the rate of £5 a week I was making in England.

Having re-established myself in Canada and the United States of America, the dreams for the future have been fulfilled. Employed in the field of aerospace engineering and contributing to aircraft design, defence systems and space programmes, my wife and family have become respected and wealthy. We have five children, all successful, and as a family have achieved full acceptance on both sides of the Atlantic where our work has proved to be beneficial.

I am surprised that, after all these years, I am sought after for interviews and talks and feel humbly proud to be one the few remaining Second World War Spitfire pilots.

Appendix

Record of Service of Flying Officer Kenneth Bosworth Johnson (143663)

Date of Birth: 5 December 1922

Non Commissioned Service:
Enlisted as No 1232125, Aircraftman 2nd Class,
    Aircrafthand Pilot/Observer, in the Royal
    Air Force Volunteer Reserve and mobilised   24 February 1941

Remustered under training Pilot and reclassified
    Leading Aircraftman   9 August 1941

Remustered Pilot and promoted
    Temporary Sergeant   18 April 1942

Discharged on appointment to a Commission   12 February 1943

Appointments and Promotions:
Granted an emergency commission as Pilot
    Officer on probation in the General Duties Branch,
    Royal Air Force Volunteer Reserve   13 February 1943

Flying Officer (was substantive) on probation   13 August 1943
Confirmed in appointment
Commission Relinquished   20 February 1945

Postings:
No 2 Recruit Centre – Cardington   24 February 1941

No 4 Recruit Training Wing – Locking   11 March 1941

No 30 Maintenance Unit – Sealand   11 April 1941

Station Sealand   30 April 1941

Station Ouston   14 May 1941

Station Catterick   28 May 1941

Station Babbacombe   28 June 1941

No 13 Initial Training Wing – Torquay   1 July 1941

No 21 Elementary Flying Training School   9 August 1941

No 5 Service Flying Training School   29 October 1941

No 3 School of General Reconnaissance –
    Squires Gate   28 April 1942

No 8 (Coastal) Operational
    Training Unit – Fraserburgh   26 August 1942

Station Benson   11 November 1942

No 543 Squadron – Benson   19 November 1942

No 541 Squadron – Benson   10 March 1943

No 543 Squadron – Benson   24 April 1943

No 682 Squadron, North West African
    Air Force – Flying Duties   11 July 1943

No 2 Base Personnel Depot –
    Non-effective, sick   22 August 1943

Station Uxbridge – Non-effective, sick
    (Replaned 3 September 1943)   2 September 1943

No 8 Operational Training Unit – Flying
    Instructor (Non-operational)   7 October 1943

No 519 Squadron – Flying duties   27 April 1944

Station Eastchurch – For reselection   4 August 1944

No 519 Squadron – Flying duties   22 September 1944

Aircrew Despatch Centre – Keresley
    Grange – Pending disposal   28 November 1944

Index

INDEX